THE SPLENDOR OF

BIRDS

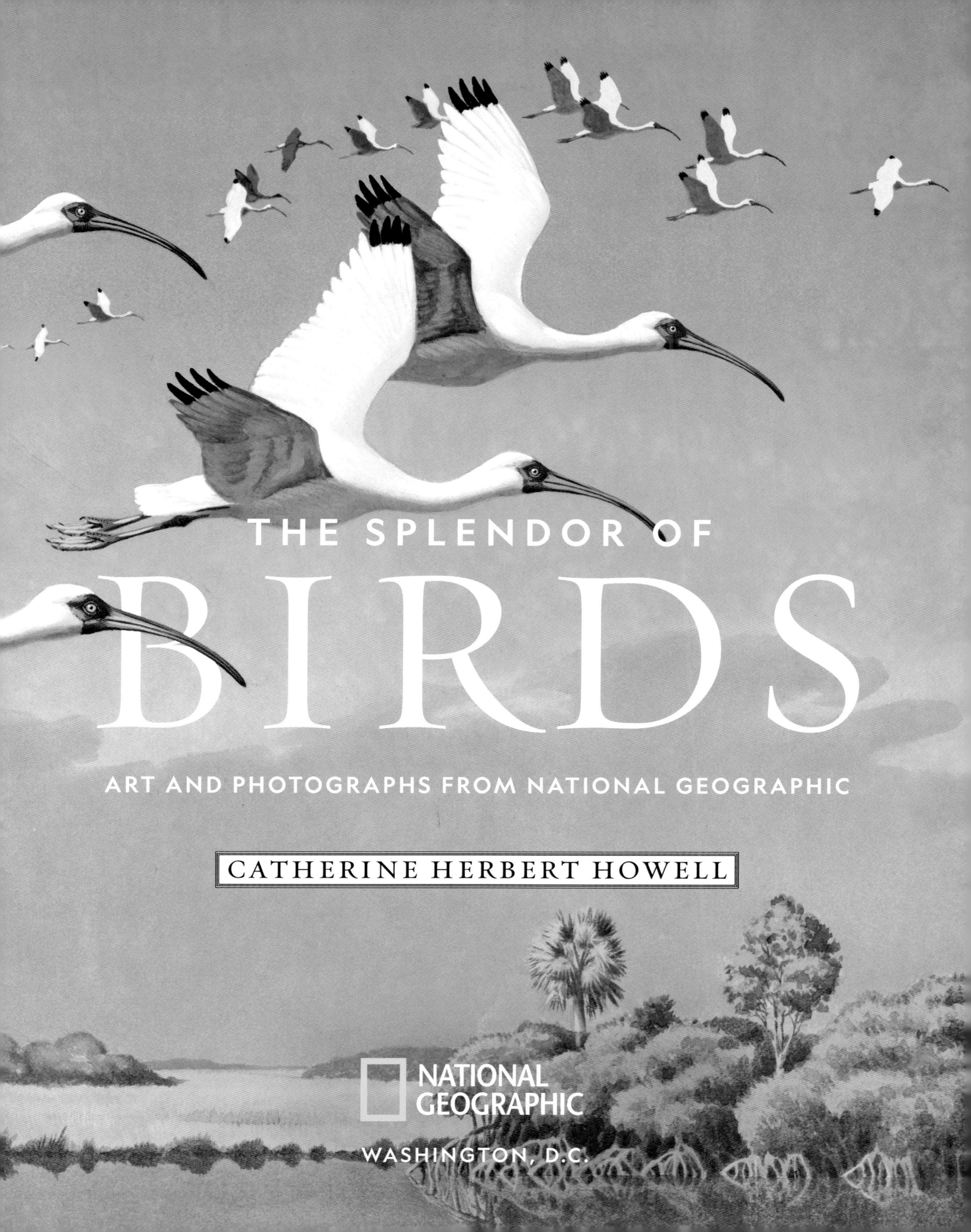

THE SPLENDOR OF BIRDS

ART AND PHOTOGRAPHS FROM NATIONAL GEOGRAPHIC

CATHERINE HERBERT HOWELL

NATIONAL GEOGRAPHIC

WASHINGTON, D.C.

H.G. PONTING,
COPYRIGHT.

CONTENTS

OPPOSITE: An Emperor Penguin poses on Antarctic ice. *Herbert G. Ponting, 1910.*

PAGE 1: A Green Peafowl surveys his elegant tail. *Joel Sartore, 2013.*

PAGES 2–3: In the evening, White Ibises head from a marsh to roost. *Walter A. Weber, 1949.*

A Snowy Owl prepares to pounce on a snow-covered mammal. *Vincent Munier, 2007.*

Flamingos lift off from an algae-covered lake on the Bolivian Altiplano. *George Steinmetz, 2008.*

Japanese women admire a domesticated white finch. *Kiyoshi Sakamoto, 1920s.*

Cobalt-winged Parakeets congregate at a pool in Ecuador to eat clay. *Tim Laman, 2012.*

A Knobbed Hornbill eats fig seeds that the species redistributes on Sulawesi, in Indonesia. *Tui De Roy, 1997.*

Godwits, with upturned bills, and Curlews, with downturned ones, appear together in a painting for comparison. *Allan Brooks, 1937.*

A male Greater Bird-of-paradise launches into his courtship display. *Tim Laman, 2012.*

A family of juvenile Northern Flickers clings to a young boy for handouts. *Lynwood M. Chace, 1933.*

The places and people that make our world are [ever] changing;
the present slips from us with growing rapidity; but the birds are ever with us.
—National Geographic, June 1913

A century ago, those evocative words from Frank M. Chapman, the famed curator of ornithology at the American Museum of Natural History, appeared in *National Geographic* magazine in an article exploring the connection between birds and happiness. More than a hundred years later, humans and birds retain their special bond. But the future of birds, and whether they indeed will be "ever with us," is no longer something we take for granted. It's something we know we must all work to ensure.

In 2018, we mark the centennial of the Migratory Bird Treaty Act in the United States, a milestone in environmental consciousness that proved legislating conservation works and that cleared the path for future federal protection, such as the Endangered Species Act. In honor of this defining moment, nature lovers around the globe joined forces to celebrate 2018 as the "Year of the Bird." National Geographic is proud to partner with leading national and international bird conservation organizations, including the National Audubon Society, the Cornell Lab of Ornithology, and BirdLife International, on this groundbreaking effort, and we are equally proud to share their commitment to champion birds for the next century and beyond.

The Year of the Bird celebration aims to raise awareness of the increasing challenges facing birds, even those in our own backyards. It also underscores the urgent need for a new, more expansive vision of stewardship, one that encompasses collaboration across borders and along flyways and that incorporates innovative approaches to protecting species and their natural habitats.

The Splendor of Birds was created both to commemorate and amplify the Year of the Bird initiative and to honor the history and wonder of these extraordinary animals. The book also gives readers an opportunity to explore the vast scope and richness of National Geographic's legendary archive. Through these luminous photographs and works of art, readers can travel into uncharted territory alongside National Geographic artists and photographers and journey through time, witnessing the growth in the world's knowledge of birds over the past 130 years and the emergence of devastating new environmental challenges.

I like to say that we have to be optimistic about the issues facing birds and other vulnerable species, but we also have to be realistic. Today, about 20 percent of the world's vertebrate species (mammals, birds, reptiles, amphibians, and fish) are threatened, and we've seen greater than 50 percent declines in vertebrate populations from 1970 to the present. Also, more than 200 of the world's bird species are at imminent risk of extinction, with many more facing critical challenges.

National Geographic has a long legacy of promoting birds and other wildlife.

Every day, we push the frontiers of science, exploration, education, and storytelling to inform millions of people across multiple platforms, including the incredibly popular National Geographic Instagram account, @NatGeo.

We also look to the past for insight and inspiration. We stand on the shoulders of sportsmen such as Henry Wetherbee Henshaw, one of the Society's founders, and photographer George Shiras 3d, both of whom set aside their rifles for binoculars, cameras, and pens in the early 20th century and, in doing so, helped shape the idea of modern environmental stewardship. It was through their vision and tireless advocacy that the Migratory Bird Treaty Act was signed into law.

Longtime Society head Gilbert H. Grosvenor was so passionate about birds that a 1943 profile of him by *The New Yorker* poked fun at how he constantly tried to slip more articles about "his favorite topic" into *National Geographic* magazine.

As the child of a bird-obsessed father and an ardent birder myself, I can relate to Grosvenor's avian infatuation. (My family spent so many holidays birding when I was growing up that my mother later warned my girlfriend to "never marry a birder.")

From the time of our founding in 1888, the National Geographic Society has funded critical scientific research projects and expeditions, awarding more than 13,000 scientific grants to bold people with transformative ideas—nearly 1,000 of which have focused on birds. The Society has also invested nearly two million dollars over the last two years alone to projects aimed at understanding and protecting birds and their migrations.

The Society funded Kristen Ruegg, an evolutionary biologist and National Geographic Explorer, who decodes unique genetic markers in the DNA of bird feathers as part of the Bird Genoscape Project. The goal of this extraordinary initiative is to harness the power of genomic sequencing to provide comprehensive, visually impactful maps of migration paths and give insight into questions such as why climate change has caused dramatic declines in some species while others remain stable.

Conservation biologist Juliana Machado Ferreira is another National Geographic Explorer driving progress. Ferreira is boldly fighting illegal wildlife trafficking in Brazil using science, advocacy, professional training, and educational outreach. The Society also supports the work of National Geographic Fellow Martin Wikelski, whose fascinating research examines bird migration and social behavior. Wikelski faced a new frontier, or what some call the final frontier, by installing equipment on the International Space Station to track data on migrating birds tagged with minuscule transmitters.

National Geographic is advancing a diversity of voices and building a pipeline of exciting ideas and initiatives, including investing in state-of-the-art technologies and innovations to help promote bird conservation under the aegis of the National Geographic Labs. We are working constantly to help create a planet in balance, one that enables the sustainability of all species and ensures biodiversity for generations to come.

Birds awe humankind with their astonishing beauty and strength. They are the most glorious and accessible ambassadors of the natural world, singing us into each new day and reminding us to pay attention to the wonder of wildlife and the interconnected web in which we live.

The earliest avian photograph in the National Geographic collection. *Charles Harris Phelps Collection, ca 1880.*

Their stories offer unparalleled examples of ingenuity and might, from the heroic, four-ounce Arctic Terns that migrate from pole to pole and back again each year (a staggering round-trip of more than 50,000 miles); to the Great Hornbills, with their massive six-foot wingspans swooping across the jungle skies of Southeast Asia; to the smoky gray-and-red Palm Cockatoos of Australia that use tools to tap out a beat to please prospective mates. Each species' tale is as singular and as remarkable as the breathtaking colors of its plumage and the spellbinding trills of its song.

Birds also give us hope. Conservation successes such as those spotlighted in *The Splendor of Birds* let us pause and celebrate. For when we see and hear stories such as the return of the majestic Whooping Cranes to Canada's Northwest Territories each spring, we marvel not only at nature's phenomenal resilience but also at the power of humankind to bring wildlife species back from the brink of extinction. This realization of what we can do if we work together strengthens our resolve to do more to save, and venerate, our wildlife and natural world.

Finally, in addition to being beacons of inspiration and joy, birds are also invaluable, irreplaceable sentinels for our ecosystem. By studying them, we can identify and address dangerous threats both to our habitat and to the planet as a whole. In this way, birds have been protecting us for years. Now it's our turn, and our responsibility, to return the favor.

I started this foreword with a quote from a legend in conservation history. I will end with the powerful words of another. Thomas Lovejoy, a renowned biologist with long and deep ties to National Geographic, once said, "If you take care of the birds, you take care of most of the big environmental problems in the world." Eloquent and urgently relevant words about these most splendorous of species. ■

—Jonathan Baillie
Chief Scientist
National Geographic Society

CHAPTER ONE

1888 —

—1939

A Balinese man holds a gamecock. *Franklin Price Knott, 1927.*

BIRDS, FROM THE BEGINNING

Birds accompany us everywhere: on mountaintops and wind-swept shores, into sun-scorched deserts, through light-dappled forests, over gentle fields, up and down urban canyons. Human cultures took note of birds early on, reflecting on their unique and awe-inspiring traits and enshrining them in myth and legend, proverb and symbolism, art and literature. Whether or not we experience them consciously, birds are an inescapable presence in our lives. Indeed, in many places, their song is the soundtrack to our lives. And they are, on the whole, beloved, by everyone from the child in the city park feeding pigeons, to the watercolor artist at his easel, to the intrepid binocular-wearing bird-watcher in the wild. It should come as no surprise, then, that in the 1880s, a fledgling organization dedicated to the dissemination of knowledge about our planet would include the avian realm in its mission.

A visual documentation and celebration of birds throughout the long history of National Geographic, *The Splendor of Birds* shows us that birds figured everywhere in the world examined, portrayed, and valued by the National Geographic Society. Birds were with National Geographic from the beginning, and they have never left. Ornithologists, wildlife biologists, and photographers (sometimes all the same individual) have followed birds all over the globe. The artists and photographers whose work is portrayed in this book have painstakingly, and sometimes at great risk to life and limb, recorded the appearance, behaviors, and travels of the planet's birdlife, often for months or even years on end. Exactly how this was done usually depended on the era: its photographic constraints, its journalistic objectives and aesthetics. The story of the avian images in this volume is a fascinating one—blending adventure, art, technology, courage (or recklessness), individual obsession, and global politics. And it has lessons for the future.

The National Geographic Society came into being on the evening of January 13, 1888, at the Cosmos Club, a gathering place for intellectual men in Washington, D.C. The 33 scholars, scientists, explorers, entrepreneurs, and military men who assembled that evening wanted to create a society expressly "for the increase and diffusion of geographical knowledge." They were an extremely accomplished group, many with careers or avocations that brought them into frequent contact with nature, and specifically birds, including Henry Wetherbee Henshaw, a well-regarded ornithologist and inveterate specimen collector destined to become the head of the U.S. Biological Survey, and Dr. Frank Baker, future superintendent of

PREVIOUS PAGES: Adult and juvenile Whooping Cranes browse in a meadow. *Louis Agassiz Fuertes, 1915.*

the National Zoo. The Society's official mouthpiece, *National Geographic* magazine, first published in October 1888, initially appealed to the academically minded. The May 1898 issue included an article about West Indian birdlife written by Frank M. Chapman, at the time assistant curator of ornithology at the American Museum of Natural History. It ran to four and a half pages and contained no illustrations. But things were about to change dramatically with the hiring of the National Geographic Society's first full-time employee.

In 1899, 23-year-old Gilbert Hovey Grosvenor, a recent graduate of Amherst College, was brought on as an assistant to the magazine's beleaguered volunteer editor. Grosvenor began his job on April Fool's Day in half a rented room in downtown Washington. He proved to be a quick study, coming up with sound ideas that were usually backed by Society president Alexander Graham Bell. Taken under "GHG's" nurturing wing, the magazine was "finally issued on time," according to Bell, who became Grosvenor's father-in-law upon his marriage to Bell's daughter Elsie later that year. Bell would recommend to the Geographic board his son-in-law's promotion to Society director and managing editor. Assuming those posts in 1903, Grosvenor wasted no time in making the contents of the magazine more popular and accessible, and setting the Society and its mission on a new path.

An avid photographer himself, Grosvenor heavily promoted photography in the magazine. When a congressman turned photographer named George Shiras 3d showed up at National Geographic's spiffy new headquarters with a box of wildlife photographs he had shot in the woods of Michigan's Upper Peninsula, Grosvenor went all in. He published 74 of the images, accompanied by minimal text, in the July 1906 issue of the magazine. Many of the images are night shots obtained by jacklighting, a hunting technique in which a light is used to disorient an animal momentarily so that it can be shot—the deer-in-the-headlights effect. Shiras also used the method of remote triggering, in which an animal trips a wire that triggers a flash and the camera shutter's release (*page 34*), an innovation that won him the nickname Grandfather Flash.

The response from Society members and the public alike was overwhelmingly positive. The issue even drew rave reviews from the nation's conservationist in chief, President Theodore Roosevelt, who immediately dashed off a note to Shiras imploring him to "write a big book . . . do it!" There was serious pushback from some National Geographic board members, however, who thought photographs distracted from the magazine's serious purpose. Two members resigned in a snit, complaining that Grosvenor was turning the magazine into a "picture book." Nevertheless, GHG held his ground.

George Shiras brought much more to the table than captivating wildlife photographs. When he served in the U.S. House of Representatives from 1903 to 1905, he had introduced the first comprehensive legislation to protect migratory birds. It didn't pass—it didn't even come up for a vote—but the much-needed bill and Shiras remained in the conversation for more than a decade. Congressman Shiras was also responsible for the creation of several national parks and wildlife refuges. Of equal significance, he was a sportsman who had taken up wildlife photography as merely a hobby, but after seeing species nearing extinction from unregulated hunting, he became a convert to hunting with a camera instead of a gun (*page 39*).

In 1912, Gilbert Grosvenor purchased a 100-acre farm in Bethesda, Maryland, then a rural outlier of the nation's capital.

He called the property Wild Acres and reveled in its abundant birdlife, which became a focus of his family's leisure time. His son, Melville Bell Grosvenor, recounted how his father took him and his sister, Mabel, into the woods to identify a bird by its call or its appearance through binoculars, rather than shooting it from the sky. Papa Grosvenor would also pay his offspring 25 cents for each wren house they built into which a wren family moved. Wild Acres attracted so much birdlife that when Henry W. Henshaw, by then chief of the U.S. Department of Agriculture's Biological Survey, toured it in 1915, he arranged for a survey there of nesting pairs; it counted 59 pairs of various species in a single acre of the property, a remarkable number then and now. Naturally, Grosvenor's obsession with birds spilled over into the magazine he edited, and the trickle of bird-oriented coverage soon became a torrent.

In those years, Henshaw had been growing ever more concerned about the plight of migratory bird species. A half century before, Passenger Pigeons had migrated in flocks of millions that darkened the sky and took hours to pass overhead. Their abundance made them too-easy targets for hunters, however. In 1914, a single captive bird was all that remained, and it would die that year. Working with his friend George Shiras 3d, Henshaw had fought for the 1913 Weeks-McLean Act that was based on Shiras's 1904 proposed bill. Among other restrictions, it banned spring hunting and the interstate sale of illegally obtained migratory birds. The bill passed, and Henshaw was there to hand Woodrow Wilson a pen with which to sign it into law. Five years later, Shiras argued vigorously for the comprehensive federal legislation known as the Migratory Bird Treaty Act. It passed in 1918, replacing the vulnerable Weeks-McLean and strengthening protection of migratory birds. With the help of Henshaw, Shiras, leaders of the Audubon Society, dedicated ornithologists, and a network of bird-loving citizens, birds could now migrate more safely within the United States and Canada.

In his editorial role, Grosvenor saw increasing value in the popular images published in his magazine's pages—both photographs and art. He cultivated relationships with photographers, conducting shrewd bargains to build an impressive collection of stock images. To put color into the magazine, he introduced hand tinting and adopted Autochrome, an early color process invented by the Lumière brothers in Paris. Autochrome was the first viable method of color photography, but plates still required a very slow shutter speed and bright sunlight (*page 26*). As a result, the images they captured were static, and the plates themselves fragile and light-sensitive, requiring careful handling before and after exposure. Still, readers were hooked. The magazine's circulation (and the Society's membership) jumped, from 1,400 in 1899 to 74,000 by 1910, and to more than 700,000 by 1920.

National Geographic's growing commitment to photography did not preclude appreciation for representational art. Paintings of birds can do what photography usually cannot: show species in their best light, to emphasize their distinctive characteristics in the context of their usual habitats. Bird artists before and even after the age of photography, including John James Audubon, often employed the "shoot-to-study" method of obtaining specimens to use as models. Indeed, most naturalists of the era were sport hunters.

In June 1913, *National Geographic* published "Fifty Common Birds of Farm and Orchard," a 32-page article by Henry W. Henshaw. The article grew out of a U.S. Department of Agriculture circular that was gobbled up by the public within weeks of its publication earlier that year—all 200,000 copies of it. Grosvenor wanted to republish the piece, and Henshaw agreed. In "Fifty Common Birds," each species is illustrated with a painting by Louis

Agassiz Fuertes, a naturalist from Cornell University who was hailed as Audubon's successor. And although the article reveals its USDA roots by judging birds on the basis of their contribution or detriment to agriculture—did they largely eat insects or valuable grain?—it contained enough basic information about the birds to serve as a mini field guide. "Fifty Common Birds" delighted the Society's members. As Grosvenor later recalled, "There's no doubt that that article . . . marked a turning point in our Magazine. It was received with tremendous interest and approval, resulting in my printing more series like it." Indeed, he published several more installments of the "Common Birds" series and much more of Fuertes's work, including a 1920 article on falconry that depicts the savage splendor of birds of prey, before the artist's prolific career was cut short when he died in a 1927 car accident at the age of 53.

Other artists of note who met the need for bird illustration include ornithologist Allan Brooks, a World War I veteran and big-game hunter who painted hundreds of birds for a series of articles in the 1930s (*pages 88–9*). Another was Hashime Murayama, a medical research technician and artist from Kyoto, who came aboard as a staff illustrator in 1921. Murayama's renderings made ordinary species extraordinary (*page 82*). Although fish were his favorite subjects, he painted a wide range of birds during his career at National Geographic, using a vintage color palette reminiscent of the great Edo-period painter Hokusai.

Birds present particular challenges to wildlife photographers: Even when one is able to spot them, they are often tiny and far away. They move quickly and suddenly. Getting good images of them requires quick exposures, difficult for early cameras to accomplish. Photographers therefore became adept at the set-up shot, erecting artfully camouflaged feeders and platforms in areas with good light and sight lines, and providing tempting fare to attract avian models. The photographer then had to disappear, to allow birds to approach without fear. The nation's first professor of ornithology, Cornell University's Arthur A. Allen, involved his family in his photography efforts, employing his son or wife as what he called a "go-awayster." Acting on the theory that birds can't count, the assistant made a pointed exit while Allen entered a nearby blind. By this reckoning, a bird would see a human depart and assume the coast was clear.

Allen also excelled at field photography, and mounted long expeditions that captured bird voices as well as images. In 1935 he shot the first photos of a nesting pair of Ivory-billed Woodpeckers, in northeastern Louisiana, which were published in the June 1937 issue of *National Geographic* (*page 98*). Within a decade, the Ivory-bill was nowhere to be found; the last conclusive sighting occurred in 1944. The bird was doomed by the selectivity of its habitat requirements and difficulties with reproduction and chick raising. Since then there have been apocryphal sightings, but the species, sadly, is now considered extinct.

By the end of the 1930s, the National Geographic Society had taken bold steps toward defining the role it would play vis-à-vis the natural world and the avian denizens within it. Birds routinely shot for sport with guns now had lenses pointed at them, with photographers bagging images to be shared with an increasingly receptive membership. Society members were coached in methods of attracting birds to their homes and gardens, for pure enjoyment and to play their part in a thriving ecosystem. At every turn, the leaders of the era negotiated a transformation in people's view of birds as economic assets to an appreciation of birds for their own sake, always engaging and eminently worthy of our concern and protection. ■

In a Louisiana swamp, an Ivory-billed Woodpecker rests on the cap of guide J. J. Kuhn after being banded. *James T. Tanner, 1938.*

A hummingbird occupies her tiny cup-shaped nest. *William L. Finley and Herman T. Bohlman, 1902.*

Its shutter tripped remotely by a string, a hidden camera photographs a Northern Flicker at its nest hole. *George Shiras 3d, 1906.*

In Michigan, a flash captures the first image of a sleeping Great Blue Heron. *George Shiras 3d, 1906.*

Harnessed ostriches provide alternative transportation in California. *Photographer unknown, 1906.*

PRESERVING PELICANS

The pelicans of Indian River suddenly assemble from all directions as though controlled by instinct or concerted signals, and a few weeks later are housekeeping on a small island occupied exclusively by pelicans for at least seventy-five years . . . Under the wise protection of the National Audubon Society and through the foresight of President [Theodore] Roosevelt in setting aside this island as a government reservation for breeding birds, there should be little difficulty in preserving the pelican of Florida from extinction, where now they may be seen daily along four hundred miles of coast, partly filling the gap made by the almost complete destruction of the egret, the white heron, the flamingo, and the roseate spoonbill, the former victims of a woman's fashion.

—George Shiras 3d

"One Season's Game-Bag with Camera," *National Geographic,* June 1908

Pelican Island, on the Indian River in Florida, was the first federal bird reservation and a forerunner to the National Wildlife Refuge System. A young Brown Pelican in the nascent refuge displays prefeather "gooseflesh." *George Shiras 3d, 1908.*

Tails fanned, Brown Boobies fly along a Bahamian shoreline. *George Shiras 3d, 1908.*

Frigatebirds soar above the Bahamas on motionless wings. *George Shiras 3d, 1908.*

Dovekies bob on the water off Greenland's frigid coast. *Underwood and Underwood, 1909.*

A quartet of Adélie Penguins wears blizzard-tipped plumage at Cape Denison in Antarctica. *James Francis "Frank" Hurley, 1912.*

TOP: Northern Bobwhite in Florida peck at bait, triggering a camera's flash. *George Shiras 3d, 1913.*
BOTTOM: On an Italian terrace, a white peacock fans his magnificent tail to impress a peahen. *Arthur Ellis Mayer, 1913.*

A Chinese man transports his hunting raptors on a pole. *Catholic Foreign Mission Society of America, 1913.*

A man shares his sandwich with a feathered friend (a chickadee). *Louise Birt Baynes, 1914.*

A White-breasted Nuthatch plucks a treat from its benefactor's lips. *Beecher S. Bowdish, 1914.*

Peruvian Pelicans as far as the eye can see roost on one of the Lobos de Afuera Islands, off Peru. *Robert E. Coker, 1914.*

This painting of a European Starling illustrated the article "Birds of Town and Country." *Louis Agassiz Fuertes, 1914.*

A Tree Swallow perches on a leafless branch. *Louis Agassiz Fuertes, 1914.*

A snowshoeing woman in New Hampshire encounters a flock of White-winged Crossbills. *Photographer unknown, 1914.*

Hoaxed by a fake blossom, a hummingbird probes for nectar. *Louise Birt Baynes, 1914.*

TOP: A Spotted Sandpiper strolls along the shore. *Howard H. Cleaves, 1914.*
BOTTOM: A chickadee finds the tied-up suet a photographer intended as a lure. *Wilbur F. Smith, 1914.*

A handsome pair of California Quail, also once known as "Valley Quail," hides in the grasses. *Louis Agassiz Fuertes, 1915.*

A Wood Thrush checks on its young in the nest. *Alvin R. Cahn, 1916.*

A perched Barred Owl surveys its surroundings. *Alvin R. Cahn, 1916.*

1916: Some of the first Western reports of bowerbird bowers assessed the constructions as playhouses built by native children. It took time for people to realize that they were fabrications built by male bowerbirds of Australia and New Guinea to impress females. The birds construct pavilions of twigs and vegetation and decorate them with stones, bones, and other objects, sometimes featuring a certain color, such as blue or red. Males of some species bring in fresh flowers daily, arranging them just so. The bower is not so much a love nest as a stage set for highlighting the male's skills as an architect and decorator and for showcasing his dance moves. A female inspects the structure and perhaps stays for the floor show, evaluating the proprietor's worthiness as a mate. If she likes what she sees, mating occurs, and she heads off to build her own nest. *(John and Elizabeth Gould)*

2010: Bowerbirds in the 21st century follow the same basic strategies as their predecessors, but their choice of construction materials and decorative elements has expanded. Even birds in remote locations have access to local human discards and samplings of the planet's abundant circulating trash. Males now add found pieces of metal, glass, and plastic to their front "gardens," including objects such as the aluminum flashing, nylon rope, and a plastic toy soldier and elephant found in the lair of a Great Bowerbird in Australia, seen here. And even though the more eclectic assortment often produces a less tidy display, female bowerbirds continue to give high marks to the nontraditional offerings, unaware of the statement they make about habitat degradation. Perhaps it is only a matter of time before a tossed cell phone or other electronic device becomes part of the assembled mix. *(Tim Laman)*

A male Kentucky Warbler takes center stage while a female peeks through the foliage. *Louis Agassiz Fuertes, 1917.*

A Red-faced Warbler, found at high elevations, perches in a conifer. *Louis Agassiz Fuertes, 1917.*

A cat eyes its raptor colleague; both were mascots of Russia's female "Battalion of Death." *Underwood and Underwood, 1917.*

Young Loggerhead Shrikes get ready to leave the nest. *Leverett W. Brownell, 1917.*

Gulls descend on low-tide debris. *Ernst Niebergall, 1918.*

THUNDERBOLT IN FEATHERS

Many stirring accounts are current of the courage and tenacity of purpose these hawks possess, but one of the most striking is of an eyess falcon belonging to a Major Fisher, which was flown at a woodcock near Loch Eil. Both birds mounted at once higher and higher, until they were entirely lost to view, even with powerful glasses. After considerable time, however, a tiny speck was seen falling out of the sky, and the woodcock, closely followed by the thunderbolt in feathers that had struck him, fell toward the very patch of fern from which he had been flushed. Before hitting the ground, however, the hawk had again overtaken her victim and struck him stone dead in the air. After so long a chase the falcon was well fed up, and, so far as she was concerned, her master wisely "called it a day."

—Louis Agassiz Fuertes

"Falconry, the Sport of Kings," *National Geographic,* December 1920

A male Peregrine Falcon takes out a Red Grouse. *Louis Agassiz Fuertes, 1920.*

Two macaws add color to a craggy landscape. *Franklin Price Knott, 1920s.*

THEN & NOW

MEET THE ALBATROSS

1922: For centuries, the albatross has captured the imagination. These magnificent seabirds, with wingspans of up to 11 feet, are the ultimate loners of the avian world. Young albatrosses can spend 10 years aloft over open ocean before returning to land to breed. With the exception of sailors in the Pacific and inhabitants of the islands where the birds nest, most people never see an albatross, and their mysterious nature has made them the stuff of legend. Maritime lore generally equates the albatross with good luck. Samuel Taylor Coleridge's *The Rime of the Ancient Mariner* recounts the tale of a sailor who kills one, an act that results in a cascade of misfortune. The two sparring albatrosses in the photo were caught with a hook and line. Lacking space on deck for a running takeoff, they remained aboard as captives, subject to bouts of seasickness like human sailors. *(William J. Peters)*

2007: A Wandering Albatross flexes its formidable wings in preparation for takeoff near South Georgia Island. Once in the air, it may travel hundreds of miles a day, perhaps gliding for hours without flapping its wings. The species does not migrate in the sense of traveling from point A to point B, but an individual can rack up more than 100,000 miles of meandering flight in a single year. Albatrosses are also famously long lived. In January 2018, a Laysan Albatross known as Wisdom returned to her breeding ground on Midway Atoll and produced a single chick to raise with her current mate; she is verified to be 67 years old. The legendary bird has produced 35 or so offspring and has outlived a number of mates. She may even have flown up to three million miles since 1956, enough for six round-trips to the moon. *(Yva Momatiuk and John Eastcott)*

Egrets and a heron blend with the serene aesthetic of a Japanese lotus garden. *Herbert G. Ponting, 1923.*

The injured Pacific Golden-Plover "Old Stump Leg" continued annual migrations from Hawaii to Alaska. *Louis Agassiz Fuertes, 1924.*

TOP: Noted for thin, flame red tail quills, a Red-tailed Tropicbird soars above Laysan Island. *Donald R. Dickey, 1925.*

BOTTOM: Sooty Terns nest on Laysan Island facing the northeast trade winds. *Donald R. Dickey, 1925.*

Unlike the piercing screams of some terns, the White Tern has a quieter voice. *Donald R. Dickey, 1925.*

PIGEONS OF THE ROYAL COURT

Probably the best-known pigeon fancier in the world to-day is King George of England, whose lofts at Sandringham contain the finest racing specimens obtainable. From those lofts birds have gone into many humble English homes, accompanied by the sovereign's best wishes, there to produce winners for their modest owners. His Majesty's grandmother, Queen Victoria, was also an ardent fancier, visiting pigeon shows whenever possible and spending many hours in her aviary . . . Thousands of years before the days of King George, another king, Rameses III of Egypt, gloried in his donations of pigeons to the temples of Thebes, Heliopolis, and Memphis. Since his time, down to the present, the Orient, especially Mohammedan countries, has regarded pigeons as sacred.

—Elisha Hanson

"Man's Feathered Friends of Longest Standing,"

National Geographic, January 1926

Victoria Crowned-Pigeons, named for the British queen, have delicate, fan-shaped crests. *Hashime Murayama, 1926.*

African Penguins storm the beaches on South Africa's Dassen Island. *Harry Pidgeon, 1928.*

A Naxi man in China holds a beautiful Lady Amherst's Pheasant. *Joseph F. Rock, 1928.*

An immature Bald Eagle perches in the enormous family nest, which weighs about a ton. *Francis H. Herrick, 1929.*

American Black and Mottled ducks, at right, evolved from the green-headed Mallard, at left, with his mate. *Allan Brooks, 1934.*

Two White Storks perch on the town ramparts of Taroudant, Morocco. *Marcelin Flandrin, 1935.*

A prized peacock wins special attention at a Connecticut animal farm. *Luis Marden, 1935.*

A Sharp-shinned Hawk on a snag creates a study in texture at a California sanctuary. *Spencer R. Atkinson, 1935.*

THEN & NOW

WILLOW PTARMIGANS

1936: Some animals that remain active in winter in snow-covered habitats undergo a change of appearance to blend in with the scenery. This occurs in some of the northern grouse species known as ptarmigans, which have mottled plumages of brown, black, and white in summer. Ptarmigans include Alaska's state bird, the Willow Ptarmigan, shown in the foreground in this painting by Canadian ornithologist and artist Allan Brooks. Small differences help distinguish the three ptarmigan species. Willow Ptarmigans display black tail feathers. Rock Ptarmigans also have black tails, and the male shows a black stripe from bill through eye. White-tailed Ptarmigans, at rear, lack these distinctive features. Their black bills and eyes are the only interruptions to their snowy winter plumage. Brooks created a companion painting of these species in summer plumage. *(Allan Brooks)*

2013: A lifetime spent in northern regions has given photographer Michael S. Quinton a unique view into the challenges faced by wildlife during long, cold, snowy winters. "I love winter!" he exclaims, adding that "the snow covers up all that distraction, simplifying the composition." And few compositions could be as spare or as simplified as this portrait of a Willow Ptarmigan. A white bird photographed in close-up against a pristine background becomes an artistic study in elegant curves and subtle shadings. The stoic arch of its neck gives a sense of the fortitude needed by each individual bird to survive in the unforgiving Alaskan wilderness. Quinton, a self-taught photographer who bought a 35-mm camera with his first paycheck, has made similar demands on himself, moving with his family to Alaska from his home state of Idaho to pursue his vision. *(Michael S. Quinton)*

A gamecock lets out a crow in Mississippi, back when the birds were raised for fighting in Gulf Coast states. *J. Baylor Roberts, 1930s.*

Whooping Cranes, at right, faced extinction in the 1930s, while Sandhill Cranes, at left and above, fared better. *Allan Brooks, 1937.*

SPYING ON IVORY-BILLS

Gradually the birds became somewhat accustomed to our presence and we dared build a blind in the top of a rock elm on a level with the nest and only twenty feet away. It was a thrilling experience to sit and listen to the conversations and watch at such close range the exchange of courtesies as these strikingly beautiful birds changed places on the eggs. The brilliant scarlet crest of the male, the gleaming yellow eye, the enormous ivory-white bill, the glossy black plumage with the snowy-white lines from the head meeting in the glistening white of the wings are as vividly pictured in my mind as if I were still sitting on that narrow board in the tree-top, not daring to shift my weight and feeling it gradually bifurcating me with wedgelike efficiency.

—ARTHUR A. ALLEN

"Hunting with a Microphone the Voices of Vanishing Birds,"

National Geographic, June 1937

A nesting pair of Ivory-billed Woodpeckers prepares to switch places at the nest hole. *Arthur A. Allen, 1937.*

Six different storm-petrel species bob offshore from a lighthouse. *Allan Brooks, 1938.*

A canary quintet occupies the same cage. *Allan Brooks, 1938.*

Northern Gannets scout for food above Bass Rock, in East Lothian, Scotland. *Niall Rankin, 1938.*

Allen's strategically placed nest box lured an Eastern Bluebird to a hollyhock blossom that complements his plumage. *Arthur A. Allen, 1939.*

Hungry young Cedar Waxwings receive insects and cherries carried in their parent's throat. *Arthur A. Allen, 1939.*

Swans and other waterbirds greet visitors at a Buenos Aires zoo. *Maynard Owen Williams, 1939.*

OF A FEATHER

THE ART OF BIRDS

BY ITS VERY NATURE, representational bird art must incorporate both aesthetics and science. To nail down details of plumage and characteristic poses, artists must understand how a bird is put together—and how it moves. Knowledge comes from direct observation and photographs, the study of preserved specimens, and dedication to the craft. Journalist T. Donald Carter once observed his friend Walter A. Weber at work in central Africa in the 1950s: "Walt would record every nuance of color and form with fast, sure strokes . . . Even in the shade of a tent fly the thermometer rose repeatedly to 113°F, and perspiration often fell onto the sketches from Walt's face."

TOP: Male and female Canvasbacks survey a frosty scene. *Louis Agassiz Fuertes, 1915.*

OPPOSITE: An illustration depicts the parts of a falcon for an instructional article. *Louis Agassiz Fuertes, 1920.*

Fig. 1

Chart, giving the Falconer's names for the parts of a hawk

Omit from plate

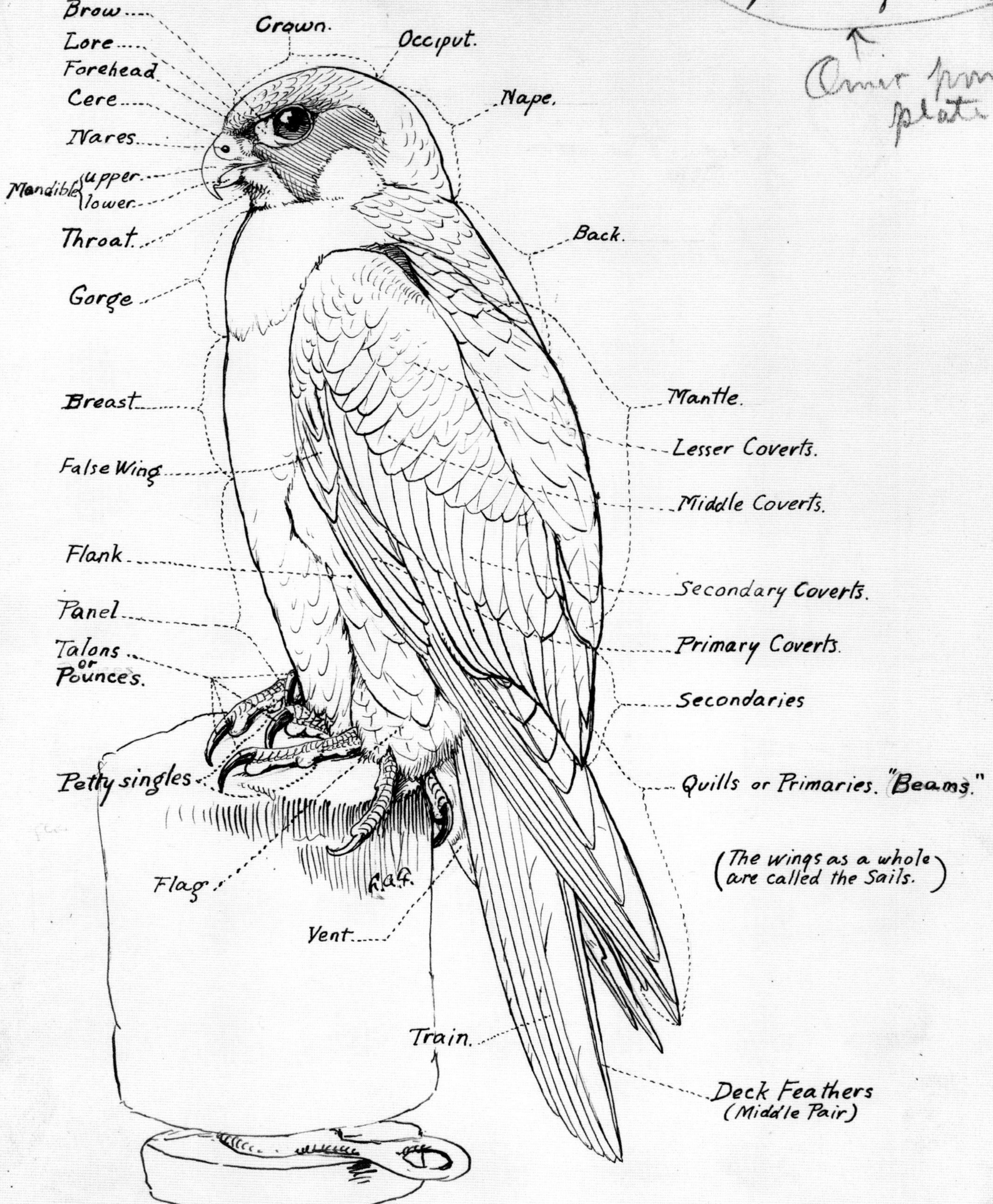

7"

5 1/6

TOP: Fruit-doves of South Pacific islands display vibrant plumage. *Hashime Murayama, 1925.*
BOTTOM: A kingfisher, cuckoo, and Red-tailed Tropicbird represent diversity among Polynesian birds. *Hashime Murayama, 1925.*
OPPOSITE: Plumage variation in Indian Peafowl is caused by sex (peacock, right; peahen, left) and selective breeding, as seen in the white birds. *Hashime Murayama, 1930.*

TOP: California Condors, now critically endangered, command the heights. *Allan Brooks, 1933.*
BOTTOM: Red-bellied and Golden-fronted woodpeckers share an oak tree. *Allan Brooks, 1933.*
OPPOSITE TOP: Swallow-tailed Kites grace a southern swamp. *Allan Brooks, 1933.*
OPPOSITE BOTTOM: Varieties of chin-strapped geese include the Cackling Goose and the larger Canada Goose, second from the right. *Allan Brooks, 1934.*

Allan Brooks

BOVE: Anhingas nest amid encircling Wood Storks in he Everglades. *Walter A. Weber, 1949.*

GHT: Two male Violet Turacos of West Africa spread heir wings to impress a female. *Walter A. Weber, 1956.*

Sunbirds from Africa sip nectar and eat small insects from poinciana blossoms. *Walter A. Weber, 1956.*

CHAPTER TWO

1940–

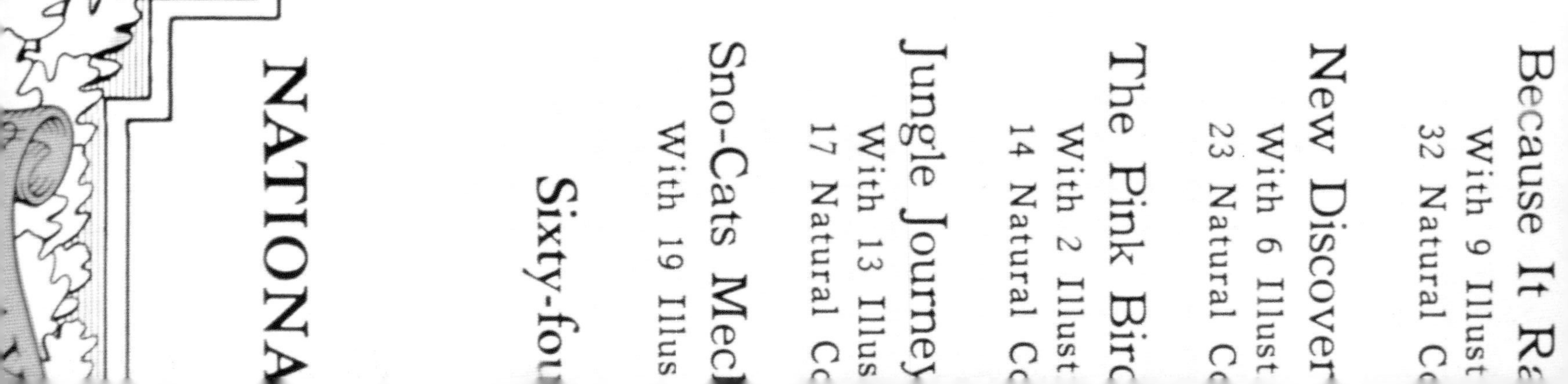

—1969

A flight attendant holds a pair of Scarlet Macaws, the mascot of TACA Airlines. *Luis Marden, 1946.*

FAR AND WIDE

As the distribution of *National Geographic* expanded, readers across the globe looked to the articles to feed their curiosity about the world, including identical twins who lived within a stone's throw of Society headquarters, John and Frank Craighead. Influenced by Louis Agassiz Fuertes's 1920 article on falconry, they applied self-taught skills to the training of different species of hawks they trapped themselves. The Craigheads were still teenagers when, as John recalled, "with halting steps and anxious glances Frank and I entered the National Geographic Society building . . . with a manuscript and a stack of pictures under our arms illustrating our experiments in training hawks and falcons to hunt for us." To the twins' astonishment, their story and images were accepted, and published in 1937—and the brothers were on their way to a career that would make them regular contributors to *National Geographic* for decades. Half a world away, a young maharaja's brother, read the article and wrote to them about his own falconry experience. A friendly correspondence sprang up, and eventually the young aristocrat invited them to see his birds for themselves. National Geographic sponsored the brothers' unforgettable trip, which became the 1942 article "Life with an Indian Prince." The Craigheads went on to obtain twin Ph.D.s from the University of Michigan and enjoy distinguished careers in conservation. Over the years they would write 13 articles for *National Geographic,* make films and television specials, and receive more than 30 research grants.

World War II interrupted Gilbert H. Grosvenor's dedicated celebrations of the world's birds. Bird coverage in the magazine declined during that conflict, and what there was took different forms. Exploits by conscripted pigeons and other birds involved in the war effort were reported regularly. A 1941 article described the care and training of homing pigeons at Fort Monmouth, in New Jersey, depicting the birds at work and hanging out after hours with their soldier caretakers (*pages 128–9*). As for the adventures of civilian birds, international expeditions in search of rare and beautiful species were suspended in favor of elaborate overland ramblings around North America.

Author-photographer Arthur A. Allen mounted expeditions that produced a series of bird articles for the magazine. The July 1943 piece "Birds on the Home Front," for example, documented the species "that the boys have left behind." Poultry and other domesticated birds also got more than their fair share of coverage in *National Geographic* during this period. Farm birds were locally available for photo ops and also figured in wartime efforts to boost food production at home.

The National Geographic Society did not go untouched by the effects of World War II. In a particularly dark period of the organization's history, the talented staff

PREVIOUS PAGES: African birds line up for a geography lesson "taught" by the Pin-tailed Whydah, at right. *Paul A. Zahl, 1953.*

artist Hashime Murayama fell victim to the xenophobia targeting persons of Japanese ancestry and was dismissed. He was interned with his family intermittently during the war but was able to receive an exemption from further internment based on his work as a medical researcher and illustrator, painting cervical cancer cells for the doctor who would go on to create the life-saving Pap test. Murayama continued to work as an illustrator after the war, but his days among the fish and birds at National Geographic had ended. Walter A. Weber, a prolific painter who traveled far and wide in pursuit of his art, replaced Murayama as staff illustrator in 1949, and held that position until 1971.

National Geographic's international coverage picked up after the war. A fascination with vibrant, exotic birds was mirrored in the color photography of the time. Smaller cameras and Kodachrome film were starting to make field photography easier, allowing photographers to travel much lighter and work on the fly. Kodachrome, with its intense color palette (thanks to complicated processing), seemed to beg for images with splashes of bright color, particularly reds. And in the realm of bird photography, what could be more colorful than a multihued parrot? A parrot held by an attractive female wearing red, of course—a photographic "get" that would become a National Geographic meme, part of the "red shirt" school of photography. Perhaps no one captured it better than Luis Marden, an early adopter of Kodachrome, who literally wrote the book on the topic, *Color Photography with the Miniature Camera*. Marden was also responsible for many advances in underwater cameras, working in collaboration with Jacques Cousteau, which opened a window onto the life of seabirds. His career with National Geographic spanned 64 years and is the stuff of legend, never to be replicated.

Photographic advances also allowed for better capture of even particularly flighty subjects, such as hummingbirds. To get a nonblurry shot, a photographer needed both a camera (still or motion picture) that operated faster than conventional ones and a rapid, bright flash that shed enough light. In the postwar years, Harold E. "Doc" Edgerton, an MIT professor also known as Papa Flash, regularly shared his work on the strobe in *National Geographic* articles, such as "Hummingbirds in Action" and "Freezing the Flight of Hummingbirds."

Hummingbird motion kept other photographers and innovators busy as well—as it still does today. Crawford H. Greenewalt, by day the president of DuPont and a National Geographic board member, transformed in his off hours into an obsessively dedicated and globetrotting photographer of hummingbirds (*page 179*). While other shooters were taking advantage of lighter weight equipment, Greenewalt packed 250 pounds of specialized gear that he had developed with his associates. He sometimes flew in the tourist section of planes while his equipment traveled in first class, as he logged 100,000 miles throughout the Americas in pursuit of his tiny subjects.

The changeover in 1957 to the editorship of Melville Bell Grosvenor, son of Gilbert H., was a watershed moment for the way *National Geographic* handled photography. MBG, as he was called, began to attract versatile photojournalists, many with newspaper backgrounds. Their more story-driven approach to the subjects they were shooting, infused with artistic sensibilities, affected the tone of the magazine's stories. As editor, MBG led coverage into controversial issues, including chemical pollution, illegal wildlife trafficking, and human evolution. What became known as the "Geographic eye" would become firmly established in the coming decades. What did this mean for birds? Less bird eye candy for eye candy's sake and more journalistic coverage of the behavior and perilous plights of many species.

Frederick Kent Truslow, a businessman who turned wildlife photographer at the age of 53, published a series of articles on international wildlife, focusing on species in various states of endangerment, including Whooping Cranes, Trumpeter Swans, and Bald Eagles. Truslow was fortunate to be working at the time the single-lens reflex camera came into wide use. With an SLR, the image seen through the lens is the image captured. Together with higher-speed films and portable telephoto lenses, SLRs allowed wildlife photographers to zoom in close for charismatic and personal shots.

As photographers and research grantees pursued stories in parts of the world previously undocumented by Western journalists, they often returned with novel revelations. Expeditions into New Guinea in the 1950s resulted in rare documentation of the courtship rituals of the elusive birds-of-paradise and the species' cultural significance in the indigenous villages with which they shared the remote rain forest (*pages 152–3*). Famed ethologist and chimpanzee expert Jane Goodall and her husband at the time, Dutch photographer Hugo van Lawick, were in Tanzania on a National Geographic–sponsored expedition when they witnessed Egyptian Vultures using stones to break eggs and recognized that this behavior met the scientific criteria for tool use (*pages 200–201*).

In the mid-1960s, the National Geographic book division, then known as Book Service, obtained the services of a who's who of ornithology, birding, wildlife photography, and art to produce two comprehensive books on birds: *Song and Garden Birds of North America* (1964) and *Water, Prey, and Game Birds of North America* (1965). MBG himself supervised the preparation of the volumes, which were filled with personal essays, historical overviews, species and bird family accounts, and thematic chapters on topics such as migration and conservation. Recordings of bird voices on flexible vinyl records accompanied each book. The books were lavishly illustrated with photographs, and with art by stalwarts such as Louis Agassiz Fuertes, Allan Brooks, and Walter A. Weber.

One of those books would soon make an unexpected impact. National Geographic had a special relationship with the U.S. space program, chronicling the achievements of the many NASA missions. When the Apollo 11 crew was tasked with designing a patch to commemorate their mission, astronaut Jim Lovell suggested the Bald Eagle as its main focus. His colleague Michael Collins perused a copy of *Water, Prey, and Game Birds of North America* and traced an eagle by Weber for the basis of the design. After a few tweaks, Weber's bird became immortalized on an embroidered patch for flight suits, jackets, and other Apollo 11 gear, and as a silkscreened image on the spacesuit worn when Neil Armstrong climbed down onto the moon's dusty surface on July 20, 1969, carrying with him a small National Geographic Society flag.

In a time bracketed by the upheaval of a world war and the mind-bending first moonwalk, National Geographic offered inspiration, information, and diversion in equal measure, while continuing to use its influence to promote a global perspective. Wildlife, including birds, remained a central concern, one that evolved as the Society evolved. It would soon no longer be enough to document—now it was crucial to deepen understanding by observing behaviors over time and finding the connections among living organisms. ■

A flushed Northern Harrier, formerly known as a Marsh Hawk, flies out of the reeds in Wyoming. *Frank Craighead, Jr., 1940.*

EAGLET ANTICS

It was often many hours between feedings, and the eaglets invented amusements to while away the time. I saw them clutch at imaginary prey with their talons, and the male enacted a fierce struggle with a dead stick, clawing and biting it. He pounced on the stick, sprang back as if in alarm, then pounced on it again and hobbled about with the stick tightly clenched in his feet. Finally, when he had disposed of it with a few quick snips of his beak, he flapped his wings, raised high his golden head, and screamed victoriously. At least I assumed that it was a scream of victory, but it was very weak and plaintive for such a large, fierce bird.

—Frank Craighead, Jr., and John Craighead
"In Quest of the Golden Eagle," *National Geographic,* May 1940

Near Laramie, Wyoming, a juvenile Golden Eagle struggles to maintain balance on John Craighead's shoulder. *Frank and John Craighead, 1940.*

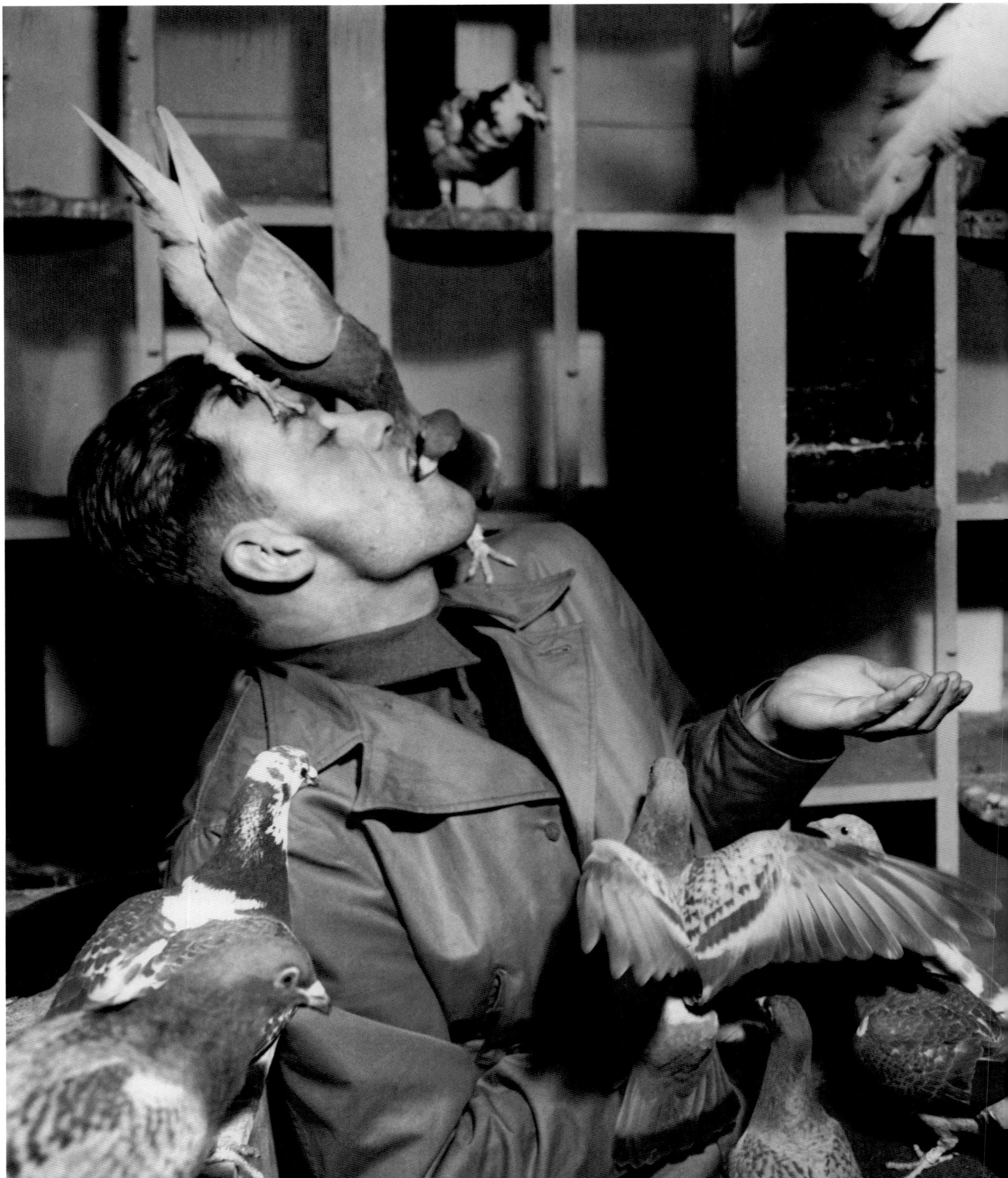

Caretaker soldiers and homing pigeons socialize in mobile pigeon barracks at Fort Monmouth. *J. Baylor Roberts, 1941.*

TOP: Girls of the Chocó people of lowland Panama and Colombia spend time with parrots. *Luis Marden, 1941.*

BOTTOM: A woman in Trinidad admires a colorful Red-and-green Macaw. *Luis Marden, 1942.*

An American Redstart comfortably feeds its family on a human perch. *Arthur A. Allen, 1943.*

The only puffins in eastern North America, Atlantic Puffins nest in rocky burrows from coastal Maine northward. *Cleveland P. Grant, 1943.*

A nocturnal frogmouth of Australia relies on its camouflage of barklike plumage by day. *Otho Webb, 1944.*

A pink Major Mitchell's Cockatoo boosted the morale of World War II soldiers serving in the Solomon Islands. *Charles L. Barrett, 1944.*

THEN & NOW

FOWL SHOTS

1944: Chickens were common on American farms for centuries, but were raised largely for eggs, not meat. That changed dramatically with the coming of World War II, when red meat was rationed, but fowl was not. The federal government encouraged the public to aid the war effort by raising backyard chickens along with their Victory gardens, to stave off a food shortage and provide sustenance for struggling Allies. The War Food Administration commandeered entire chicken production plants to send to the armed forces, and eventually even German POWs were shipped to the United States to work the poultry farms and maintain supply. This turkey, part of a 4,000-bird flock raised in Idaho's sagebrush country, got a last cuddle before doing his part for the troops as Thanksgiving dinner. After the war ended, industrial chicken farming helped make poultry the leading meat consumed in the United States. *(Maynard Owen Williams)*

2016: Domesticated fowl descend mainly from the handsome Red Junglefowl, still thriving in a wide range over southern Asia and some Pacific islands. In addition to barnyard chickens and roosters, Junglefowl gave rise to the birds used in cockfighting, a spectator pastime that has been practiced for centuries in many parts of the world. In those cultures, specially bred fighting cocks are highly valued, and their sparring matches, resulting in gore and often death, are big business, generating significant wagers. Cockfighting now draws opposition for its violence and cruelty toward animals and has been outlawed in many countries and in all 50 U.S. states. It is still legal, and culturally entrenched, in the Dominican Republic, though, where this youth lives. The bird he proudly displays wears plastic spikes that augment its own spurs, making them even more lethal in matches. *(Lynn Johnson)*

The miniature scale of fledgling Elf Owls is put into perspective by the hand of an intruder near their perch. *Lewis W. Walker, 1945.*

At maturity, a juvenile male Redpoll like this one will acquire a rosy breast. *Arthur A. Allen, 1945.*

TOP: A Black-billed Cuckoo watches the first chick emerge from its clutch of blue eggs. *Arthur A. Allen, 1945.*

BOTTOM: Mission accomplished! A Belted Kingfisher displays its fishing success. *Arthur A. Allen, 1945.*

Blue Jay nestlings excitedly anticipate the meal their returning parent transports in its throat. *Arthur A. Allen, 1948.*

Swallow-tailed Kites perform aerial maneuvers over Everglades wetlands. *Walter A. Weber, 1949.*

The delicate courtship plumage of Snowy Egrets pops against the dark waters of a mangrove swamp. *Walter A. Weber, 1949.*

Northern Gannets rest on the cliffs of their rookery on Bonaventure Island, Quebec. *John E. Fletcher, 1949.*

THE PINK BIRD OF TEXAS

Courtship in this colorful species begins in early spring and is almost as exotic as the bird's appearance itself. Spoonbills returning from a winter of dispersion usually begin to congregate on specific islands in April. During the preconnubial period one may observe some very interesting exhibitions of mass behavior. Sometimes a wading group, quite undisturbed by outside influences, will burst skyward in unison, circle for a while, and then settle again. Sometimes all the individuals of a wading group, again in seeming mechanical unison, will point their beaks skyward and gaze rigidly into space for long periods. When the hypnosis suddenly breaks, the birds lower their heads and proceed with normal feeding activities. It is during this period of odd mass behavior that pairing occurs, accompanied by elaborate stick play between the sexes. Male and female are almost identical in external appearance; it is only by their actions that the observer may distinguish between them.

—Paul A. Zahl

"The Pink Birds of Texas," *National Geographic,* November 1949

A Roseate Spoonbill uses its wings to balance as it lands on a branch in a gust of wind. *Paul A. Zahl, 1949.*

A plump male California Quail displays a pair of adjacent, identical, teardrop-shaped black head plumes. *Paul J. Fair, 1950.*

This Twelve-wired Bird-of-paradise, named for its black, wirelike tail feathers, lived more than 20 years in captivity. *New York Zoological Society, 1950.*

WALTER A. WEBER

Two male Emperor Birds-of-paradise compete for female attention. The display starts with perching and ends upside down. *Walter A. Weber, 1950.*

THEN & NOW

FROZEN IN TIME

1951: When it comes to flight, hummingbirds have a gymnastic skill set. They can fly forward, backward, sideways, and up. They can also hover—and not just for a few moments, like Ospreys and kingfishers, but for 30 seconds at a time. Extremely well-developed chest muscles facilitate this hovering, as does an enlarged heart. The ability to rotate wings generates lift on the upstroke of the wing as well as the downstroke. Documenting birds' reverse flight—once regarded by some as an optical illusion—required capturing the motion of wings that can beat up to 200 times per second, depending on the species. Dr. Harold E. Edgerton and his colleagues created high-speed stroboscopic lighting synchronized to a camera shutter. The strobe froze motion intermittently, proving over three exposures how a female Broad-tailed Hummingbird could back away from a feeder. *(Harold E. Edgerton, R. J. Niedrach, and Walker Van Riper)*

2017: The secrets of Hummingbird flight continue to be revealed, thanks to greater knowledge of ornithology and to the technological advances that afford ways to set up tests and document behavior that lies beyond the power of human observation. Researchers routinely put hummingbirds through their paces, as in this aerial obstacle course set up by photographer Anand Varma; it is designed to replicate maneuvers through the dense vegetation of branches and vines that hummingbirds must negotiate in forests without breaking their lightning speed. A narrow, oval aperture mimics natural circumstances and induces hummingbird acrobatics. To get through the hole, the bird shimmies sideways, altering its wing strokes to avoid contact with the hole's edges. This frame combines three exposures captured in .4 second, hence the circular opening appears to cut through the bird as it emerges. *(Anand Varma)*

Terns swarm past Longstone Lighthouse in the Farne Islands, off England's northeastern coast. *J. Allan Cash, 1952.*

Babe, a Great Hornbill, plucks a cherry from a keeper's mouth at the London Zoo. *B. Anthony Stewart and David S. Boyer, 1953.*

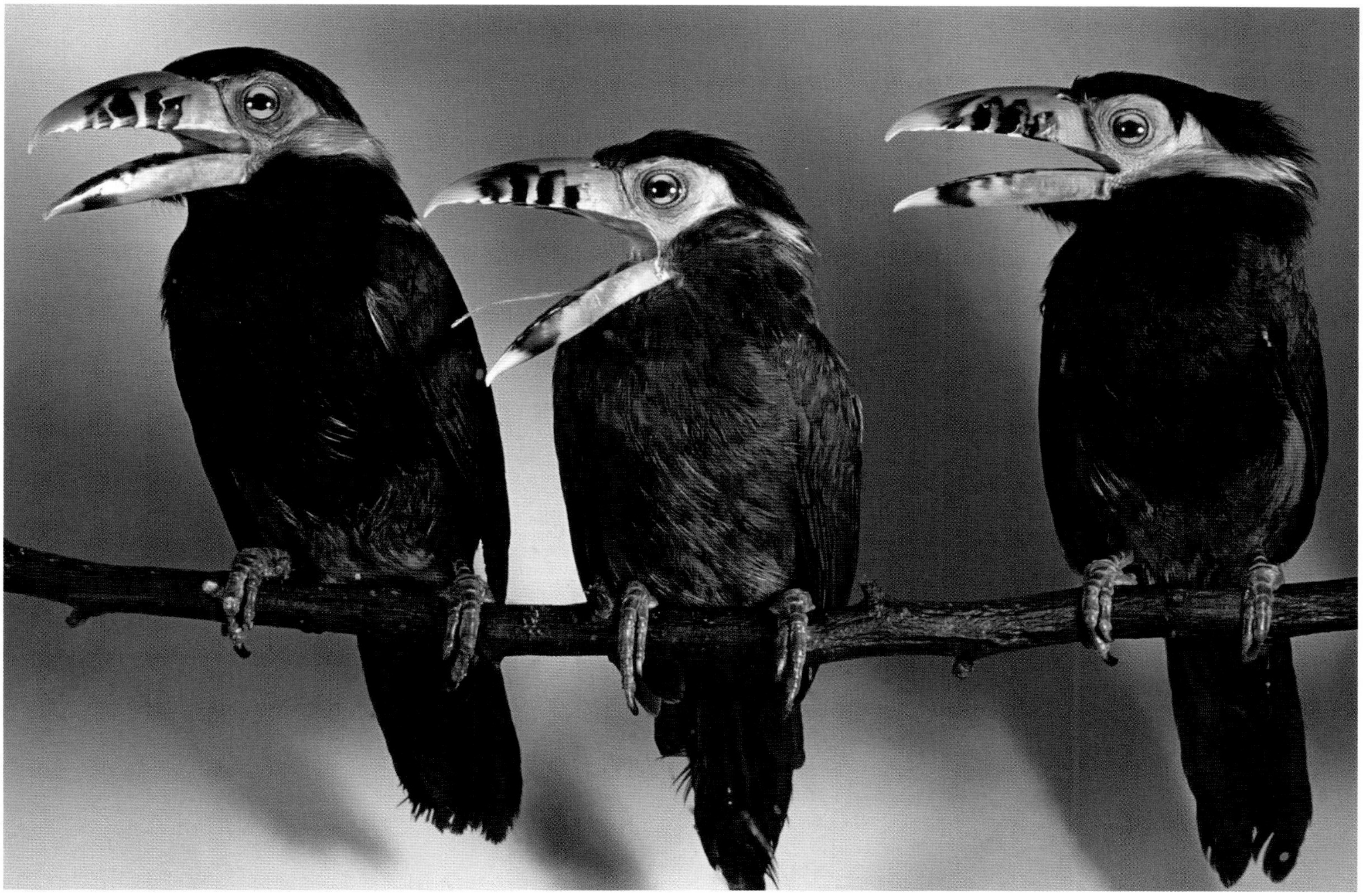

Photographer Paul A. Zahl likened the squawk of the Spot-billed Toucanet to “ripping canvas.” *Paul A. Zahl, 1953.*

These honeyguide species of Africa and Asia feed on various bee products, including beeswax. *Walter A. Weber, 1954.*

A female Greater Honeyguide considers laying her egg in the nest of Violet-backed Starlings. *Walter A. Weber, 1954.*

A trio of White Ibises pauses motionless in tall marsh grass in a Texas refuge. *Robert F. Sisson, 1954.*

A rare California Condor spreads its majestic wings into a nine-foot span above its cliffside perch. *Carl B. Koford, 1954.*

Soaring through Florida skies, a flock of Wood Storks displays airborne grace. *Allan D. Cruickshank, 1954.*

A Common Chaffinch lights on the hand of the caretaker of Wordsworth's Dove Cottage, in England. *David S. Boyer, 1956.*

TOP: A flamingo smooths ruffled feathers by rubbing its long neck across its wings. *B. Anthony Stewart, 1957.*
BOTTOM: The massive bill of a Keel-billed Toucan weighs little more than an ounce. *Robert F. Sisson and Donald McBain, 1957.*

A richly hued shining-parrot perches on the limb of an imported breadfruit tree in Fiji. *Luis Marden, 1958.*

Western Gulls swarm the wake of a boat in the Santa Barbara Channel, foraging for scraps from its galley. *Bates Littlehales, 1958.*

A Black-crowned Night-Heron in southern Spain's coastal marshes, known as Las Marismas, displays long white head plumes. *Roger Tory Peterson, 1958.*

Guanay Cormorants congregate on the rocks on Don Martín Island, off the coast of Peru. *Robert Cushman Murphy, 1959.*

NOT-SO-MUTE SWANS

Nine hundred years ago, as now, across the brackish waters of the Fleet, myriad terns would have swooped above Chesil Beach. The abbot of the now-vanished Benedictine monastery that began the swannery would probably have asked how many cygnets were to spare for the roasting spits . . . At present the swannery's 35,000 animal visitors feast only with the eye. It is something to reflect that spring after spring for hundreds of years has been heralded by the swans, gliding two by two from their winter breeding grounds five miles away. Around us on the marsh we could count half a hundred ramshackle heaps of stick-and-reed nests built by the industrious swans. The air was clamorous with parental concern. "Mute!" said Fred scornfully. "A mute swan can make at least eight different sounds." Therewith he mimicked a range from a twangy trumpeting to an alarm call (Fred transcribes it as "Herbert! Herbert!"), a defense call, and a cry of victory.

—Michael Moynihan

"The Swans of Abbotsbury," *National Geographic,* October 1959

A female Mute Swan leads her brood of cygnets through a narrow ditch, with the male bringing up the rear. *Barnet Saidman, 1959.*

The wing and tail feathers of Common Ostriches on a South African farm are destined for hats and dusters. *W. D. Vaughn, 1960.*

Racing against rising waters, a Black-necked Stilt builds up one side of her nest to try to prevent flooding. *Frederick Kent Truslow, 1960.*

A hummingbird called a Brown Inca showers under a small waterfall in Ecuador. *Crawford H. Greenewalt, 1960.*

Flocks of pigeons are nearly as iconic as the domed basilica in Venice's Piazza San Marco. *John Scofield, 1961.*

HONEY, I'M HOME!

When the on-guard bird spotted its returning mate, it practiced an important rule of stork etiquette. Flinging its head backward until the crown touched its back, the bird rattled its big red bill noisily. Then, throwing its head forward with a stiff, formal bow, it rattled some more. The returning adult also began to clatter. The duet built to a climax. Bowing and head throwing were accompanied by tail cocking and pirouetting with half-open wings. This rigid greeting ceremony is a sort of mutual courtesy that probably strengthens the bond between the pairs. However, storks, unlike geese, do not mate for life. Banding shows that while the birds may return to a nesting site, they usually change partners annually.

—Roger Tory Peterson
"White Storks, Vanishing Sentinels of the Rooftops,"
National Geographic, June 1962

A stork bander gently uses a rake to coax White Storks from a false chimney at a Dutch inn. *Volkmar Wentzel, 1962.*

Hoatzins perch in a tree in Guyana. Scientists still debate the classification of these unique birds. *M. Woodbridge Williams, 1962.*

Ducks at the Bronx Zoo get a lot of human attention—and tasty snacks. *Albert Moldvay, 1964.*

A parrot is presented to a parrotfish through a porthole of the Continental Shelf Station Two, an experimental underwater habitat for aquanauts in the Red Sea. *Robert B. Goodman, 1964.*

THEN & NOW

ANCIENT ANCESTORS

1964: It all started with a single feather. In 1860 a worker at the Solnhofen quarry in southern Germany discovered a perfectly preserved feather in a limestone slab. The find, which dated back 150 million years, seemed too good to be true but checked out as authentic, and was soon followed by others: partial and full fossils of a small and birdlike creature with a feathered body and wings. In 1861 the dinosaur was named *Archaeopteryx lithographica*, and it has captured the public's imagination ever since. At the time of its discovery, Darwin had just published *On the Origin of Species* and was delighted that the feather bolstered the case for evolution. Since then, the challenge of re-creating the dinosaur's appearance in life and the flight potential of its wings has been taken up by many artists, including famed illustrator Roger Tory Peterson. He depicted the crow-size animal both perched and in a glide. *(Roger Tory Peterson)*

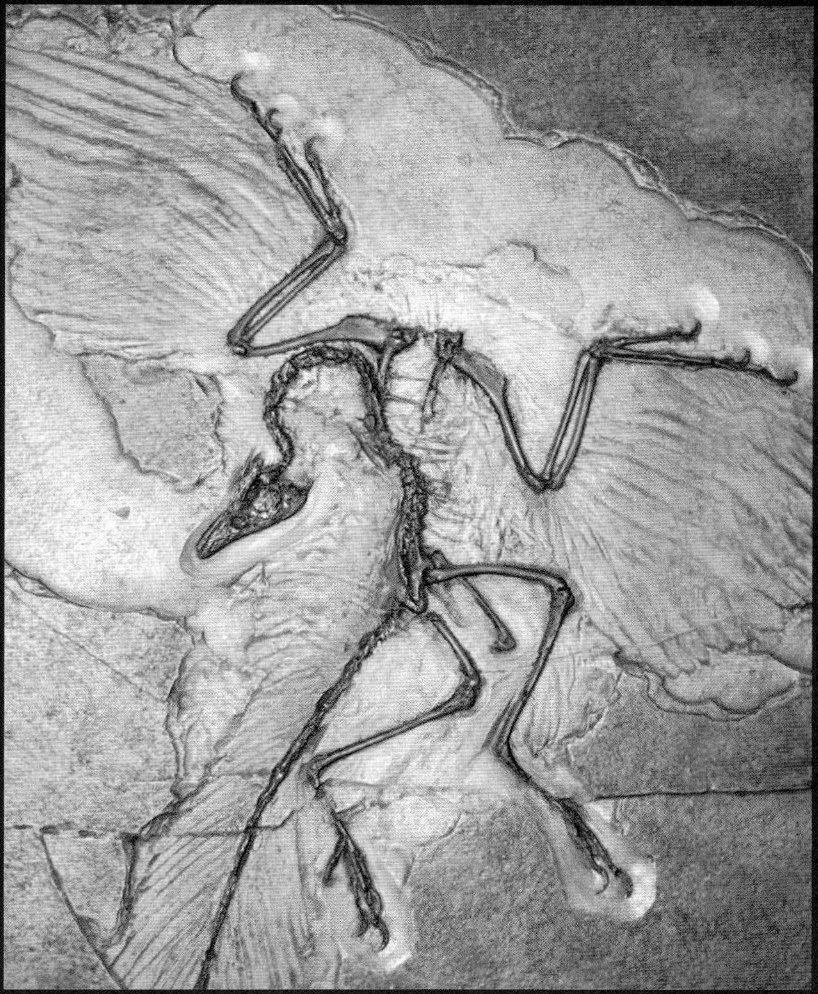

2006: Since the 1860s, only a dozen complete *Archaeopteryx* fossils have been discovered, and each received a nickname, usually based on where it ended up. The Berlin fossil, discovered in 1876, is a prized artifact of that city's Humboldt Museum of Natural History. Unlike today's birds, this fossil shows a long, bony tail and a predator's sharp teeth. Details continue to emerge on the appearance, function, and evolution of feathers and flight. One of the most fertile fossil fields is in China, where a number of finds in recent years seem to have knocked *Archaeopteryx* squarely off its prehistoric pedestal as contender for "first bird." Scientists now know that feathers predated flight, which suggests that the creatures used wing and tail feathers for balance while leaping after prey or gliding short distances and for insulation or visual displays. Even the famous *Tyrannosaurus rex* was likely covered in feathers. *(Jason Edwards)*

This hovering Oilbird in Peru bounces echoing clicks off cave walls in order to navigate. *Edward S. Ross, 1965.*

A Great Egret in Florida preens the long, decorative feathers of its breeding season plumage. *Frederick Kent Truslow, 1965.*

Florida's Dry Tortugas islands are the only nesting location in the lower 48 for the Brown Noddy, a wide-ranging tropical tern. *Otis Imboden, 1965.*

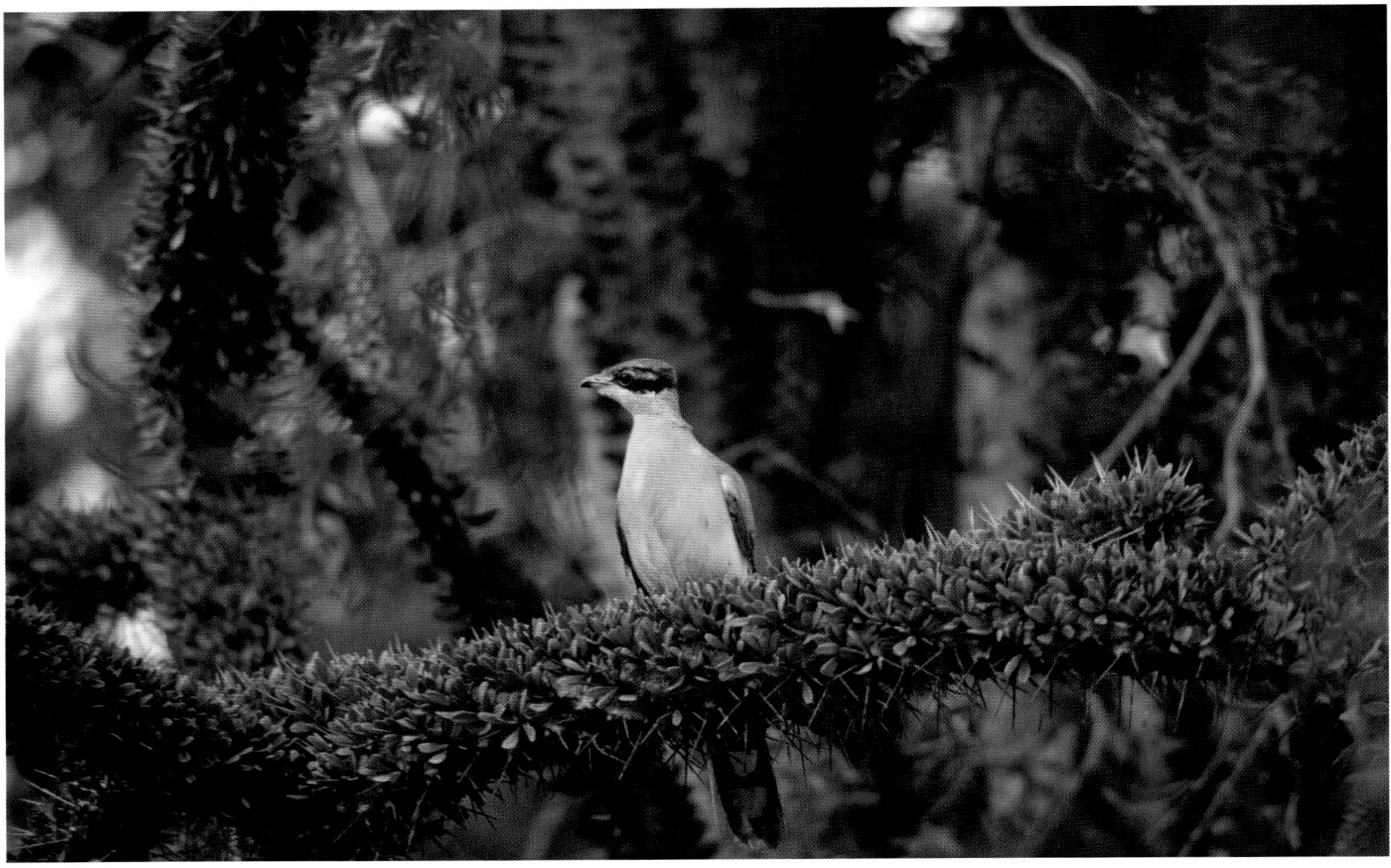

TOP: The rising sun silhouettes a roosting Great Egret in Everglades National Park. *Otis Imboden, 1967.*
BOTTOM: A Green-capped Coua perches on an *Alluaudia* tree in Madagascar's spiny desert. *Luis Marden, 1967.*

A Scarlet Flycatcher hunts insects in the Galápagos Islands. *David S. Boyer, 1967.*

Canada Geese rise off a field after a breakfast of corn at Crab Orchard National Wildlife Refuge in Illinois. *James L. Stanfield, 1967.*

Caged goldfinches ride home from market on the head of an Afghan woman in Kabul. *Thomas J. Abercrombie, 1968.*

Two species of colorful lorikeet chow down on their delivered breakfast in Queensland, Australia. *Winfield Parks, 1968.*

A LUCKY DISCOVERY

"He's using a tool!" Hugo and I exclaimed almost with one voice. Amazed, we watched an Egyptian vulture, a white, yellow-cheeked bird about the size of a raven, pick up in his beak the stone he had just thrown down. The bird raised his head and once more threw the stone at the ostrich egg lying on the ground before him. It was true! We were watching that seldom-recorded phenomenon—the use of a tool by an animal. And we were, as far as we know, the first scientifically qualified witnesses to this extraordinary talent of the Egyptian vulture . . . There are, however, other birds that do use tools. The Galapagos woodpecker finch probes grubs from their holes with a small twig or cactus spine held in the beak. The satin bowerbird of Australia is reported to use a wad of bark when painting the inside of its bower.

—JANE GOODALL

"Tool-using Bird: The Egyptian Vulture," *National Geographic,* May 1968

An Egyptian Vulture on the Serengeti Plain tries to break a fake egg with a stone in an experiment to observe tool use. *Hugo van Lawick, 1968.*

A farmer herds a flock of ducks down a rural lane in Bali. *Donna K. and Gilbert M. Grosvenor, 1969.*

Reclusive Rufescent Tiger-Herons live in the wet lowlands of Central and South America. *Frank and Helen Schreider, 1969.*

OF A FEATHER

HATCHLINGS & JUVENILES

THE CHARACTERISTICS OF A BIRD'S early life depend on its species. Some birds are precocial—that is, fairly well developed at birth. Ducks emerge alert, covered in down, and able to follow Mom to water soon after. Precocial species tend to fare better than the weak, featherless, helpless hatchlings of altricial species, such as sparrows. The location of hatching also makes a difference. Offspring of ground-nesting species, for example, face greater peril than those hatched in tree cavities. The juvenile period in altricial cases can be short or long, depending on the species. Large raptors, such as Bald Eagles, can take several years to reach full adult appearance.

TOP: A Herring Gull chick that recently hatched from its egg sits in a Lake Superior island nest. *George Shiras 3d, 1906.*
OPPOSITE: A young Tricolored Heron gets its first leg band. *Howard H. Cleaves, 1914.*

TOP: Removed from its nest, a Greater Roadrunner devours a long lizard its mother had just delivered. *William L. Finley and Herman T. Bohlman, 1932.*
BOTTOM: A male Cooper's Hawk and his bigger sister stare down the photographers. *Frank and John Craighead, 1937.*
OPPOSITE TOP: Google-eyed Least Bittern hatchlings point bills upward in an attempt to look fierce. *Arthur A. Allen, 1939.*
OPPOSITE BOTTOM: A Hoatzin chick has claws on its wings that disappear in adulthood. If a predator approaches, the chick can drop out of the nest to take cover and then claw its way back home. *M. Woodbridge Williams, 1962.*

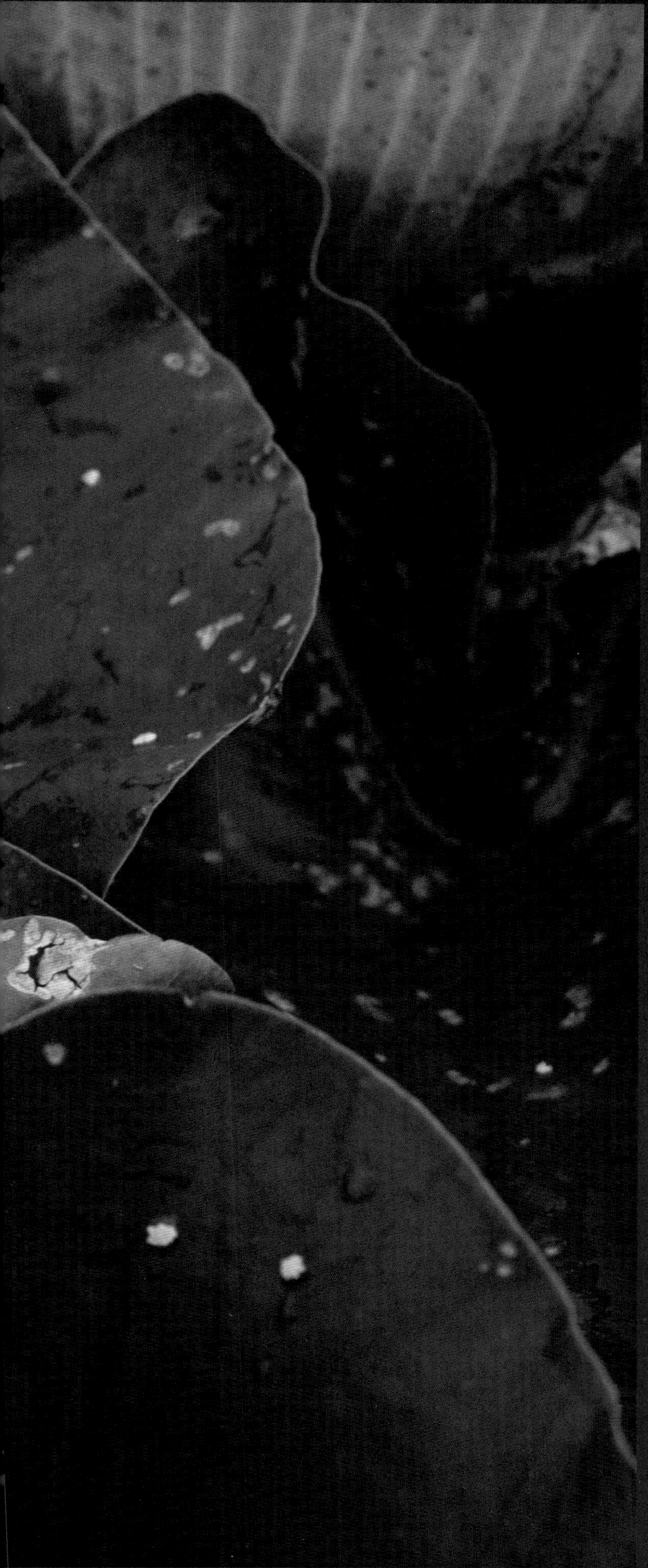

LEFT: In Alaska, an hours-old Trumpeter Swan cygnet rests on a pond lily. *Art Wolfe, 1985.*
TOP: An ostrich hatchling in Tanzania totters away from unhatched eggs. *Mitsuaki Iwago, 1996.*

TOP: Tall grasses help conceal a juvenile ground-hornbill in Botswana's Okavango Delta. *Vincent Grafhorst, 2010.*
BOTTOM: A juvenile Harpy Eagle flexes its wings to threaten a passing vulture. *Tui De Roy, 2010.*
OPPOSITE: A fluffy young booby wanders from its nest in Australia. *Paul Chesley, 2010.*
NEXT PAGES: Frigatebird chicks await circling adults on Rawaki Island, in the central Pacific Ocean. *Brian Skerry, 2011.*

CHAPTER THREE

1970 —

— 1999

Sarus Cranes in India posture during a mating ritual. *Stanley Breeden, 1976.*

AS THEY LIVE

The first Earth Day was celebrated on April 22, 1970, a signal of new awareness of the planet's fragile ecology, and the impacted wildlife within it, that morphed into an international yearly recognition. Also in that watershed year of 1970, Gilbert M. Grosvenor, son of Melville Bell Grosvenor, took over as editor of *National Geographic* and began to promote what he later called "better stewardship of the planet" within the magazine's mandate. Now a strong environmentalist bent influenced assignments given to writers and photographers, a match with the swelling environmental movement.

A photo by Bruce Dale in the December 1970 magazine issue, covering "Our Ecological Crisis," planted an indelible image in readers' minds of the effects of maritime oil spills on wildlife. It showed an oil-drenched Western Grebe swimming through the iridescent film of a slick created by an 11-day offshore well blowout off the coast of Santa Barbara, California. The image was one of the most persuasive calls to action of that time, and the unfortunate grebe came to represent the millions of waterbirds that would suffer similar fates worldwide in the decades to come. Recurring reports featuring volunteer rehabbers armed with nothing but dish detergent and TLC gave the impression that there was an easy fix for epic carelessness, but it was not so—such efforts could aid only a fraction of affected birds. However, the public's strong reaction to the coverage of the accident sparked a wave of new laws; more environmental legislation was passed in the next few years than at any time in U.S. history. Like the Migratory Bird Treaty Act of 1918, nationwide laws such as the National Environmental Policy Act (NEPA) and the Clean Water Act have a tangible effect on birds and other wildlife.

In this period, *National Geographic*'s readership, increasingly enamored of wildlife documentaries on network and cable television, expected and appreciated the drama of nature. Likewise, the magazine developed a kind of "street photography of the wild side." Back-garden setups of earlier decades were replaced by carefully constructed blinds in remote locations, with photographers hunkering down for the long haul—the-right-place-at-the-right-time scenarios that required no end of patience. After all, it was generally acknowledged that wildlife photography was, in the words of one early practitioner, "an occasion of lost chances." The era of pretty women with parrots was over.

Few wildlife photographers at the time were more patient than the dynamic duo of Australians Des and Jen Bartlett. Their family life was an endless safari, meticulously planned and fastidiously documented. They

PREVIOUS PAGES: Snow Geese fill the skies above Delaware Bay in New Jersey. *Bob Krist, 1981.*

waited for their photographic moments in chest-deep water, in sun-pierced desert blinds, camped out on the back of Jeeps, and exposed on the mosquito-filled tundra (*pages 220–21*). The Bartletts fairly dominated the wildlife coverage in *National Geographic* during the 1970s, producing eight articles in that decade alone, while continuing their award-winning cinematography.

Early in the 1980s, the Society made a bold decision to publish a bird field guide. The time seemed ripe for a comprehensive guide based on painted representations of birds with clearly identifiable field marks. Updating the model introduced in 1934 with the pathbreaking, birder-friendly books of Roger Tory Peterson, the enterprise required a large team that included not only expanded editorial, design, and production staff in the Book Division, but also a legion of birding experts for counsel and a stable of 13 established bird illustrators to produce 220 color plates. The level of detail involved was unprecedented.

During the three years that it took to bring this colossal undertaking to fruition, the Book Division became Bird Central. Consultants and authors such as Jon L. Dunn and the late Rick Blom roamed the halls arguing volubly the finer points of color description (a big deal in the birding world), such as the difference between "buffy-gray" and "grayish-buff." Some staff jokingly suggested that it would be helpful to have a tunnel connecting National Geographic's Washington, D.C., headquarters to the Smithsonian's National Museum of Natural History, a mile away, so frequent were the visits to the bird division there to check paintings against the skins of the minimally taxidermic birds in its extensive collection. Perhaps the biggest challenge was managing, under a tight schedule, the production deadlines for all the guide's art. Drawn into the unenviable chore of artist wrangling, one editorial staffer remarked, "The artists were professionals and very experienced, but keeping all of them motivated and productive simultaneously often required the skills of both coach and therapist."

It was a gamble that paid off. The first edition of the *National Geographic Field Guide to the Birds of North America* was published on October 25, 1983, to rave reviews, a huge accomplishment in the competitive and highly scrutinized arena of field guide publication. The book's loyal following extolls the guide's inclusiveness, clarity, and—a big plus for long excursions on foot—portability. In 2017 the field guide was revised for a seventh edition, which included a new total of 1,023 species and extensive updates (*page 267*). It was a challenge to retain the handy size while incorporating new paintings for plumage variations for sex, age, and molt; map updates to reflect greater knowledge of range; and taxonomy rearranged to match sweeping changes from the Committee on Classification and Nomenclature of the American Ornithological Society.

The *National Geographic Field Guide* would not have helped ornithologist Jared Diamond (of *Guns, Germs, and Steel* fame), who made one of the period's most famous bird discoveries while on an ecological research expedition in New Guinea funded by National Geographic and the World Wildlife Fund. While there, Diamond sighted the elusive Golden-fronted Bowerbird, then known as the Yellow-fronted Gardener Bowerbird, which ornithologists had been seeking for decades, their certainty of its existence based only on some museum skins that lacked documentation. In an eagerly anticipated November 1981 press conference, Diamond gave his take on why male bowerbirds build bowers. "The males with the dullest plumage build the fanciest bowers. It's like the dull young man with the fancy sports car," he offered.

Wildlife photography took on new possibilities in 1986 with the invention of the Crittercam, developed with National Geographic support. Marine biologist Greg Marshall got the idea for it from watching a slender fish, the remora, cling tightly to a shark's body as it powered through the water. The prototype was tested on a captive sea turtle. Since then, Crittercams have been worn by some 50 animals, both marine and terrestrial, and their initial weight has dropped from about six pounds to under two. Early models could only record, but now visual and other data can be monitored from afar in real time, and the harness can be jettisoned remotely if the wearer's well-being comes into question. In the bird realm, Crittercams have been deployed on Emperor Penguins.

Over these last three decades of the 20th century, wildlife photographers continued to bring their unique skills and backgrounds to their work, claiming niches of coverage as their signature beats. Bill Curtsinger earned his photography chops in the U.S. Navy's Photo Unit. Underwater photography therefore became his métier, and he concentrated on Arctic and Antarctic locations. Penguins and other species of the planet's cold lands and seas figure widely in his coverage (*pages 224–5*). The lenses of Dutch photographer Frans Lanting have captured the inhabitants of ecological "hotspots," some two dozen natural environments around the globe containing species found nowhere else. Lanting completely immerses himself in the ecosystem of the species he covers, spending weeks on a platform in the rain forest canopy or living in isolation on desolate atolls with albatrosses and other seabirds, who are declining at a faster rate than any other species group (*page 277*). The rewards are high. "The birds have very little fear for humans because they never see any human beings in the course of their lives," says Lanting. "That means I can get very close." His exquisite images drove home point after point about exactly what was at stake when commercial fishing, climate change, and pollution disrupt the perfect attunement of a seabird to its environment.

In 1915, Gilbert H. Grosvenor's Wild Acres, the bucolic farm he had purchased three years earlier, hosted a breeding-bird survey of a single acre of the property. Some 78 years later, National Geographic linked up with the North American Breeding Bird Survey to explore the seeming decline in bird populations in the forests east of the Mississippi. Journalist Les Line and photographer Scott Goldsmith followed naturalists with the U.S. Fish and Wildlife Service along the paths of some 200 species of migratory songbirds between eastern North America and the birds' wintering grounds in Central and South America. Instead of getting the kind of happy news Grosvenor had received—his property was bursting with nesting pairs—the naturalists learned that the songbirds of eastern forests now faced forest clearing, increased predation, and more human interference, all of which was causing a noticeable drop-off in numbers.

By the end of the second millennium, a path had been cleared for National Geographic explorers, scientists, and photojournalists to follow birds to the stories the birds themselves seemingly want to tell, in the ways appropriate to their avian lives. Birds know no borders or boundaries of the human variety. Following them to the ends of the earth or as they endlessly circle great oceans, National Geographic enables us to learn in depth about their lives and challenges, all working according to the principle that protecting these treasures wherever they may live or alight is our duty—and privilege. ■

Enjoying the catch of the day, an Osprey rips into a fish. *Des and Jen Bartlett, 1970.*

The aptly named Rainbow Lorikeet is a common visitor to Australian backyards. *Gordon Gahan, 1970.*

A pet Rose-ringed (Ring-necked) Parakeet perches on the head of a Lohar youth in Rajasthan, India. *George F. Mobley, 1971.*

Imperial Shags, aka Blue-eyed Cormorants, share prime breeding real estate with Gentoo Penguins in Antarctica. *Bill Curtsinger, 1971.*

A Cactus Wren perches among the prickles of a cholla at Organ Pipe Cactus National Monument in Arizona. *Walter Meayers Edwards, 1971.*

A Pacific Loon sits on its nest in Canada's Northwest Territories. *Des and Jen Bartlett, 1971.*

Omnivorous gulls accept handouts from boat passengers off Britain's Channel Islands. *James L. Amos, 1971.*

A male Great Curassow displays the swollen yellow bill knob that announces breeding season. *Michael E. Long, 1972.*

Young and gangly, a Tricolored Heron chick in Virginia peers above the brush surrounding its nest. *Bill Curtsinger, 1972.*

Using a pellet of bait, a Green Heron has successfully lured and caught a fish. *Robert F. Sisson, 1974.*

PELICAN PLUNGE

Aerial acrobat, the pelican uses feet and a six-foot span of powerful wings as air brakes in making a landing. But when it sights a fish, it becomes a sleek dive bomber. Head cocked, wings bent, the bird plunges, changing body attitude to keep its eye on the target. BAM! Wings and legs thrust back, neck rammed forward, the diver spears the water just after another pelican, beyond, smashes through the surface. Only after studying such pictures did the author learn that the bird's head remains fixed on the prey even while the body twists as much as 180° for aim and balance. With exceptional vision, pelicans can spot a fish and dive from as high as 75 feet. Air sacs under the skin cushion the crash. But the momentum still thrusts the bird a foot or two beneath the surface.

—RALPH W. SCHREIBER

"Bad Days for the Brown Pelican," *National Geographic,* January 1975

Diving for fish off Tarpon Key, Florida, a Brown Pelican exhibits perfect form. *Bill Curtsinger, 1975.*

In Brazil, a hermit hummingbird with a black mask drinks from the bloom of a bromeliad. *Paul A. Zahl, 1975.*

Painted Storks stand guard over their treetop nests in Rajasthan, India. *Stanley Breeden, 1976.*

A Bald Eagle flexes its majestic wings atop a snow-covered tree near Haines, Alaska. *Steve Raymer, 1976.*

Vivid Satyr Tragopans, aka Crimson Horned-Pheasants, inhabit forested Himalayan slopes. *Stanley Breeden, 1976.*

A female Magnificent Frigatebird shelters her nestling in Florida's Marquesas Keys. *Bianca Lavies, 1977.*

Taking flight, an American Avocet makes a splash at Bear River Migratory Bird Refuge in Utah. *Bates Littlehales, 1977.*

THEN & NOW

GREEN JAYS

1977: Birds of medium size and tropical coloration, Green Jays might be the least known of the corvids (crows, jays, and their kin) that inhabit the United States. The species barely makes it into the country from its more extensive range in Mexico and Central America, reaching traditionally only into southern Texas. Except in the breeding season, when they are more secretive, these gregarious birds travel about in small flocks, showing curiosity when an intruder enters the area. And being jays, they definitely have something to say about it. As a 1933 *National Geographic* article reported, "They have a great variety of harsh screaming notes, varied with a medley of caws, toots, and whistles, and for a few minutes noisily hover about the intruder from a discreet distance and then melt silently away into the bush and are seldom seen again unless deliberately followed up." *(Bates Littlehales)*

2011: Although Green Jays have a limited range in the United States, they are common enough throughout their total range that their survival status is not in question. Photographer Joel Sartore gave the jay an appointment during his studio shoot of captive animals at the Houston Zoo—and the colorful bird did not disappoint. Pursuing a lifelong project he calls the Photo Ark, Sartore has circled the globe, visiting zoos and wildlife centers to make studio portraits of animals—especially those that are endangered. But Green Jays have more than their looks going for them. They possess the hallmark intelligence of the corvid family and are documented tool users, having been observed using twigs to extract insects from underneath tree bark. They also show signs of cooperative breeding, in which an offspring cohort stays at the nest and helps raise the next generation until they fledge. *(Joel Sartore)*

A White Tern hovers over namesake Tern Island in the Northwestern Hawaiian Islands. *Jonathan Blair, 1978.*

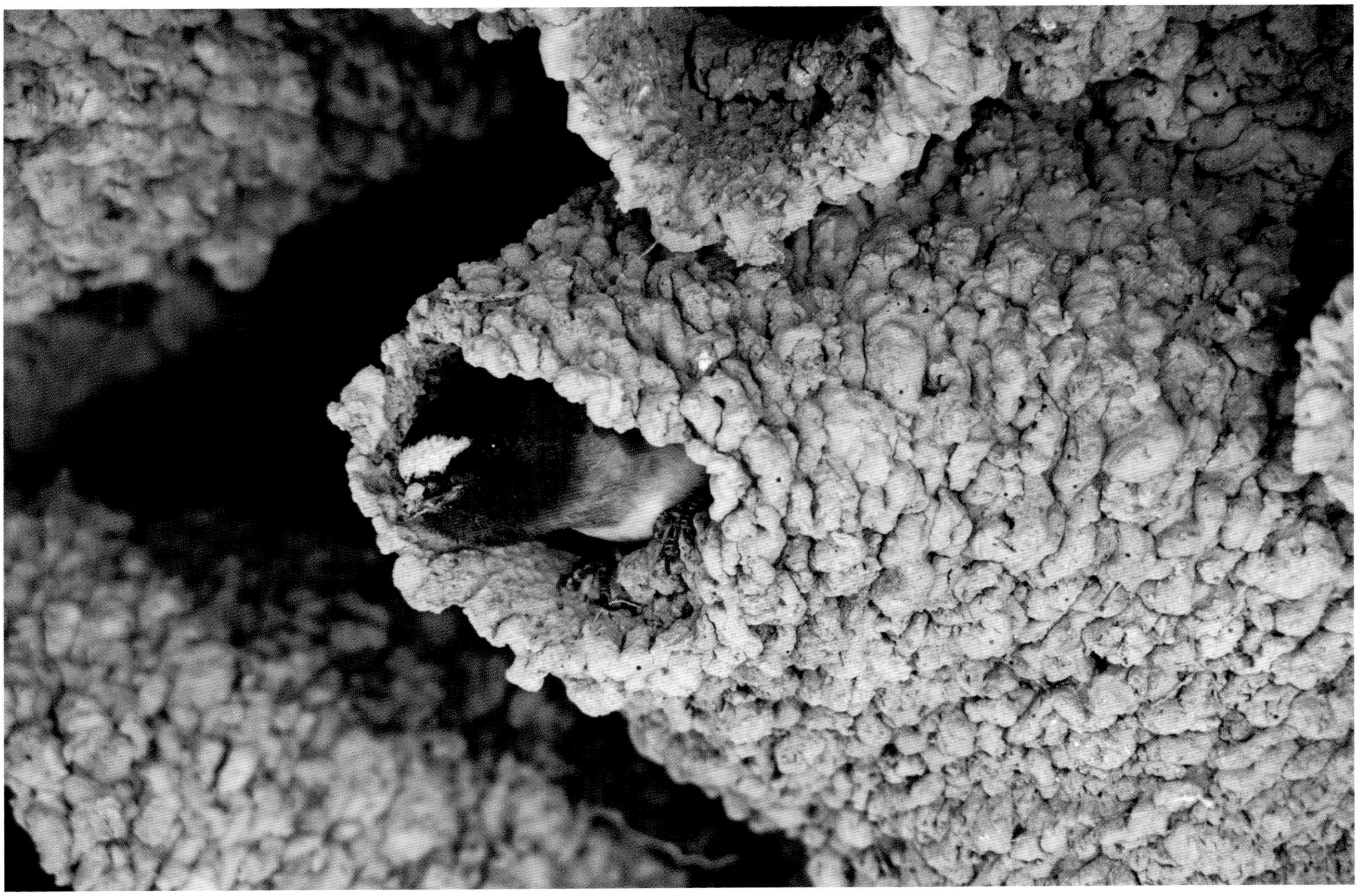

A Cliff Swallow peers from a mud nest of its own construction at a wildlife refuge in Utah. *Bates Littlehales, 1979.*

Tufted Puffins nest on the Farallon Islands, sometimes called the Galápagos of California due to the seabird diversity there. *Bates Littlehales, 1979.*

Singing his heart out, a Baird's Sparrow perches in a North Dakota wildlife refuge. *Bates Littlehales, 1979.*

TOP: A Roseate Spoonbill glides over a lagoon in Everglades National Park. *David Alan Harvey, 1979.*
BOTTOM: A flash of white wing patches helps identify a male Yellow-headed Blackbird. *Bates Littlehales, 1979.*

Poised to carry out commands, a falcon waits on the arm of a Bahraini emir's falconer. *Steve Raymer, 1979.*

EXPLAINING MIGRATION

1979: Laden with symbols reminiscent of an astrological chart, a painting hints at the factors that may guide migrating birds to their far-off destinations. The subject is a Yellow-billed Cuckoo, which travels from the central and southern United States to South America for the winter. The bird is surrounded by representations of the signals that inform its journey. Some signals are visual: the sun, stars, different wavelengths of light; others are auditory: the sound of distant surf. Concentric circles represent Earth's magnetic field, and pendulums signify gravity. Weather cues include storm fronts (the curved "banner" line) and favorable winds, while landmarks such as mountains also come into play. In the decades since this painting was created, our general understanding of bird migration has grown, with some of the most promising results emanating from the neural structures of the avian brain. *(Barron Storey)*

2013: Some three billion birds representing 300 species migrate, round-trip, between Europe and Africa each year. As this information-packed map demonstrates, the annual crossings involve four general routes, which offer shorter or longer journeys but little safety in transit. Mediterranean migrants face four basic perils, represented by blue symbols that, ironically, mimic traveler amenities on road maps: bird hunting for consumption (as a culinary delicacy) and leisure, for illegal trade, and for farm protection. Ominous dark red sunbursts represent high-kill locations. Despite international protection treaties and intense monitoring by bird advocacy organizations, the large-scale assaults continue. Countries with the highest number of flagrant offenses appear in the darker pinkish hue. *(Fernando G. Baptista, Virginia W. Mason, and Daniela Santamarina, NGM staff; Fanna Gebreyesus)*

Like schoolchildren standing at attention, Great Blue Heron chicks gather in their pine tree nest in New Mexico. *Jim Brandenburg, 1981.*

TOP: An American Flamingo family cruises a lagoon in the Galápagos Islands. *Sam Abell, 1981.*
BOTTOM: Great White Pelicans beg for fish scraps at a lake in Congo. *James A. Sugar, 1982.*

A Trumpeter Swan cuts a wake across a tranquil Yellowstone River in Wyoming. *James P. Blair, 1982.*

A Western Meadowlark sings from a field in Nebraska's Valentine National Wildlife Refuge. *Farrell Grehan, 1982.*

Black Oystercatchers traipse across a pebbled shore on Protection Island, Washington. *Bates Littlehales, 1982.*

DESERT DASH

Mexicans were calling the bird *corre camino*—"it runs the road"—long before modern highways. I have followed roadrunners along deer trails and other animal pathways that provide both an edge of vegetation for foraging and numerous insects living on animal wastes. Rather than a "beep" like an automobile horn, the bird when startled or alarmed makes a "clack" by rattling together the upper and lower parts of its bill. In all, I have identified 16 different sounds, including a cooing call during courtship and a whine by the female during nest building. Roadrunners satisfy their voracious appetites with an astonishing variety of prey. Though they occasionally eat bits of plants, their diet leans heavily toward insects, a boon to farmers. The seemingly fearless birds also feed on other birds, snails, mice, bats, scorpions, tarantulas, and black widow spiders. The diet of nestlings is almost entirely reptiles.

—Martha A. Whitson

"Clown of the Desert," *National Geographic,* May 1983

A Greater Roadrunner delivers a snake to its nestlings in Big Bend National Park, Texas. *Bruce Dale, 1983.*

TOP: A Royal Tern lands with breakfast at nesting grounds on the Sea Islands off the coast of South Carolina. *Annie Griffiths, 1983.*
BOTTOM: A Great Egret rides the tail of a gliding crocodile, snagging fish that leap to escape. *Dieter and Mary Plage, 1983.*

A Red-crowned Crane in Japan plays solo catch by tossing and snatching a corn husk. *Tsuneo Hayashida, 1983.*

THEN & NOW

FIELD GUIDE ART

1983: The art created for a field guide leaves little room for poetic license. Field guide illustrators can and do express their signature artistic styles, but in their depictions of individual birds and the details of their plumage, they must stick to the facts. Also, general bird guides today are seldom the work of one illustrator. They tap the talents of multiple artists often specializing in certain bird groups. This was the case with the 1983 first edition of the *National Geographic Field Guide to the Birds of North America,* a monumental task that involved more than a dozen artists. Their 220 plates, or paintings, depict more than 800 bird species, including the male Tufted Titmouse, at left, and the Black-crested Titmouse, right, both the work of ornithologist John P. O'Neill, also well known for his studies of neotropical birds. *(John P. O'Neill)*

2017: The seventh edition of the *National Geographic Field Guide to the Birds of North America* featured 300 new illustrations that required intense scrutiny by experts to pass the test for publication. (The argument for using art for field identification is that an artist can depict the most typical plumage, attitude, and key identifiers of an entire species, while a photograph is beholden to variables such as lighting and the characteristics of an individual bird.) Before painting commenced, preliminary sketches traveled back and forth from artists to authors to consultants. The completed paintings were then scanned and subtly color-corrected for accuracy in printing and to balance the new art with the existing art. Guide co-author Jonathan Alderfer created many illustrations for the seventh edition, including the Common Ground-Doves depicted here, both individually and compared in flight to the Ruddy Ground-Dove. *(Jonathan Alderfer)*

American Avocets pair with their mirror images in shallow water in Nevada's Black Rock Desert. *James P. Blair, 1983.*

Ground squirrel is on the menu as a Ferruginous Hawk delivers a meal to its young. *James P. Blair, 1984.*

A female Great Gray Owl keeps her fluffy owlets close in a snag in Idaho. *Michael S. Quinton, 1984.*

The nests of Openbill Storks decorate treetops in the wetlands of Rajasthan, India. *James P. Blair, 1986.*

THEN & NOW

UNDERWATER ACROBATS

1986: The pursuit of Emperor Penguins on a food foray into frigid Antarctic waters is an extreme challenge, but few come to it as qualified as Bill Curtsinger, a graduate of the U.S. Navy diving school. Curtsinger describes his historic shoot in the predigital era: "I tried for two or three years to get near Emperor Penguins underwater, and one day it all came together. I was diving at the edge of the seasonal ice in McMurdo Sound. I heard them before I saw them, but when they saw me they simply swam all around me for about ten minutes. I was able to hand my housing to my dive assistant up on the sea ice to reload my underwater cameras, so I did get more than 36 chances, maybe four to five rolls max, and then, in an instant, they were gone. I never saw Emperor Penguins underwater again." *(Bill Curtsinger)*

2012: Photographer Paul Nicklen is separated in age from Bill Curtsinger by almost a generation. Nicklen straddles the film/digital photography divide, but with every passing day, his portfolio tips more to the digital side. Nicklen, who grew up on Canada's Baffin Island, is also an experienced cold-region photographer. He braved water temperatures of 28°F to capture this image of Emperor Penguins diving in Antarctica's Ross Sea, where they descend deeper than 1,750 feet, staying under for more than 20 minutes on one breath. Nicklen doesn't have to worry about the limitations of a roll of film in a camera that can't be reloaded underwater. He explains, "With digital photography I can have several thousand images on a [memory] card as opposed to 36 on a film canister. The other difference is that I get to instantly see that my exposure is proper when working digitally." *(Paul Nicklen)*

The feet and underside of a floating phalarope, photographed from below, are reflected in the water. *Bates Littlehales, 1987.*

A Bald Eagle alights on a treetop on Graham Island, British Columbia. *Dewitt Jones, 1987.*

TOP: A soulful, cooing crooner, the Mourning Dove is a common North American species. *Bates Littlehales, 1987.*
BOTTOM: Black-browed Albatross chicks wait for parental meal delivery to their Falkland Islands rookery. *Frans Lanting, 1988.*

Dangling feet are the only sign of the chick that this Comb-crested Jacana carries tucked under its wing. *Belinda Wright, 1988.*

This South Polar Skua delivers a stern warning to a human intruder on the Falkland Islands. *Frans Lanting, 1988.*

Nepal's national bird, the Himalayan Monal, roams Sagarmatha National Park, a sanctuary for this popular game bird. *William Thompson, 1988.*

The Blue-winged Kookaburra is one of the iconic kookaburra species of Australia, known for their laughing calls. *Sam Abell, 1989.*

Folding in its wings to shade its eyes, a Black Heron tries to locate fish in Botswana's Okavango Delta. *Frans Lanting, 1990.*

A Great Egret stalks prey in the waters of a cypress swamp in the Everglades. *Farrell Grehan, 1990.*

Wood Storks and egrets share an Everglades pond. Both species are closely monitored by conservationists. *Medford Taylor, 1990.*

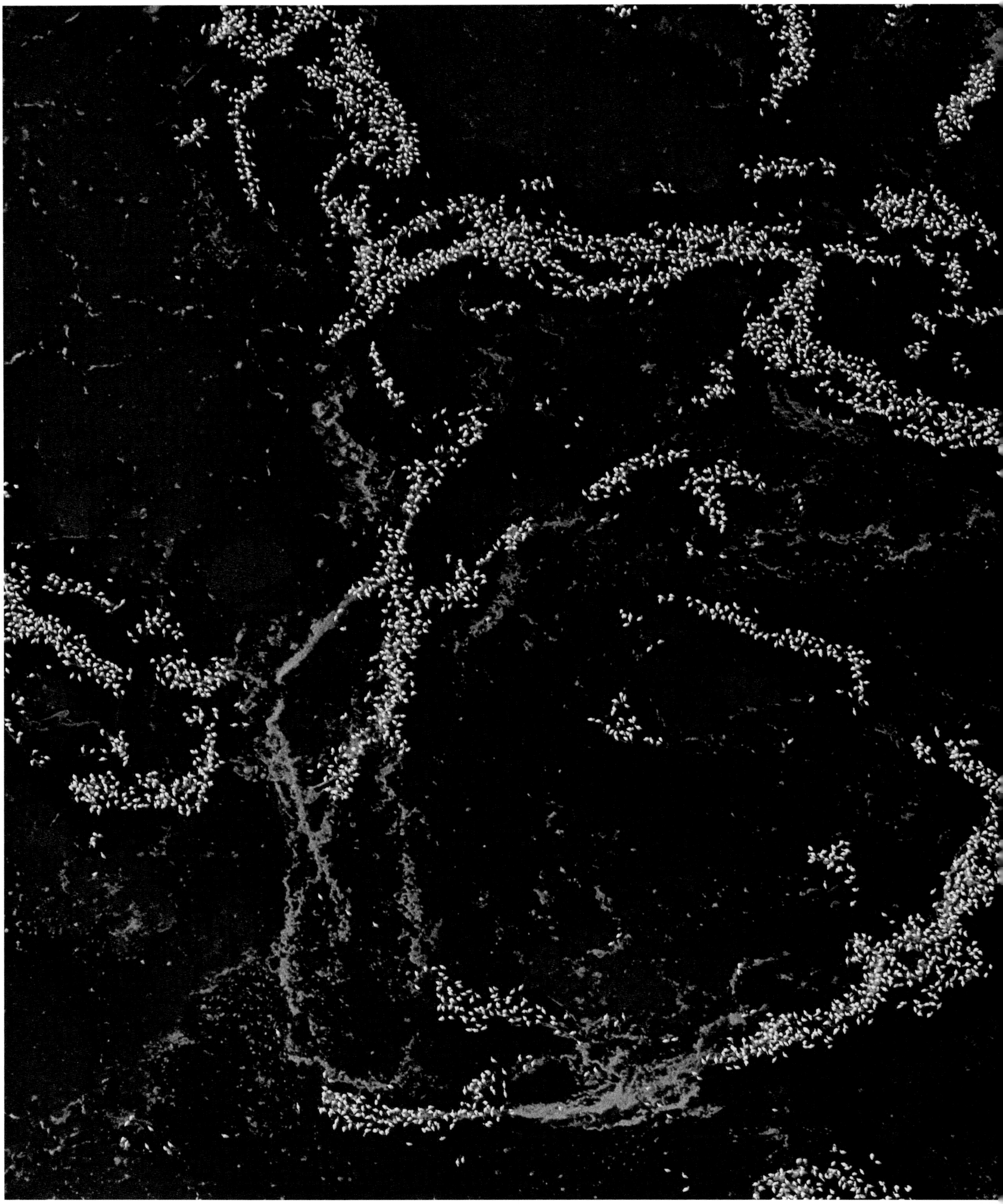

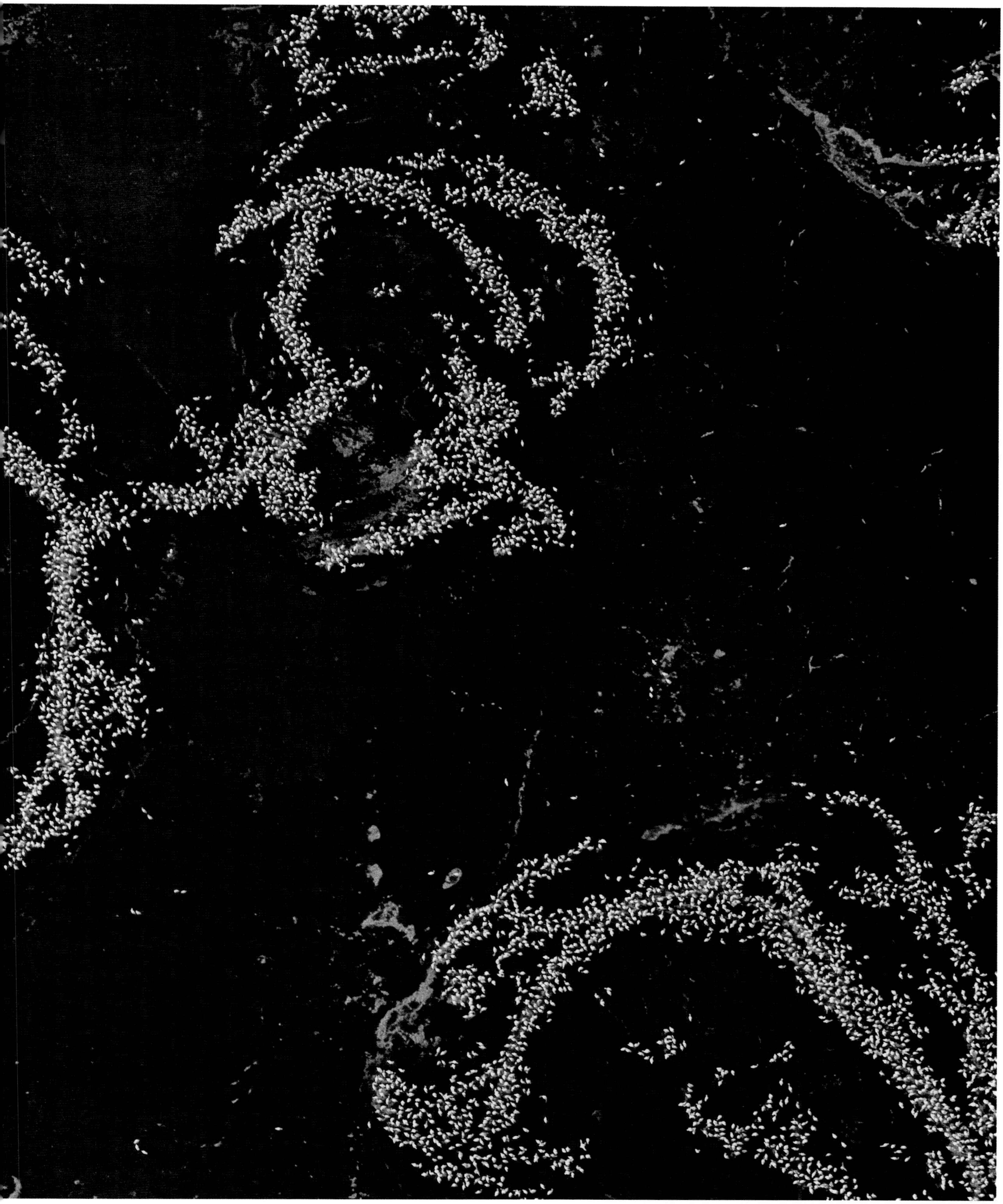

Swirls of pink mark nesting Lesser Flamingos on Lake Natron in Tanzania's Great Rift Valley. *Chris Johns, 1990.*

TOP: A pair of endangered Bali Mynas find refuge at the Bronx Zoo. *Michael Nichols, 1991.*

BOTTOM: Dappled light creates a watercolor backdrop for a Great Blue Heron in Florida. *Jim Brandenburg, 1991.*

All tucked up and standing on one leg, an American Flamingo sleeps at the Audubon Zoo, in Louisiana. *Michael Nichols, 1991.*

Silvery-cheeked Hornbills, native to eastern and southern Africa, pose at Omaha's Henry Doorly Zoo. *Michael Nichols, 1991.*

An assortment of waterbirds perches on pilings in the Chesapeake Bay. *Robert Madden, 1991.*

Canada Geese flap past the Lower Manhattan skyline toward Long Island to feed. *Raymond Gehman, 1992.*

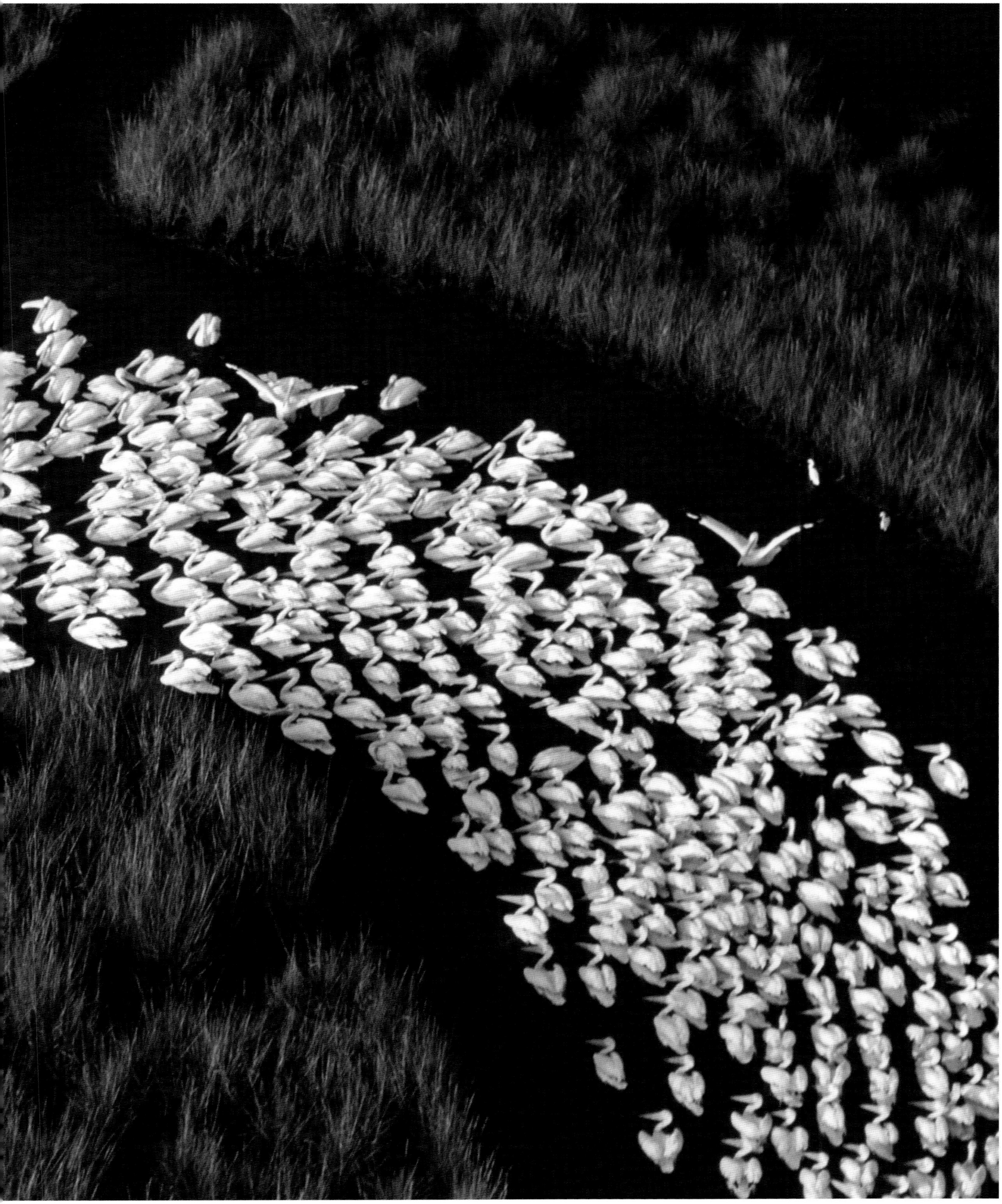

American White Pelicans create a traffic jam along a salt marsh channel in the Mississippi Delta. *Annie Griffiths, 1992.*

TOP: The Harlequin Duck thrives in white-water rapids and untamed landscapes. *Bates Littlehales, 1993.*
BOTTOM: A Nēnē, or Hawaiian Goose, an endangered species, honks amid wildflowers at Kilauea Point National Wildlife Refuge, on Kauai, Hawaii. *Chris Johns, 1993.*

A Siberian Crane chick uses oil from a gland on its back to waterproof its feathers. *David H. Ellis, 1994.*

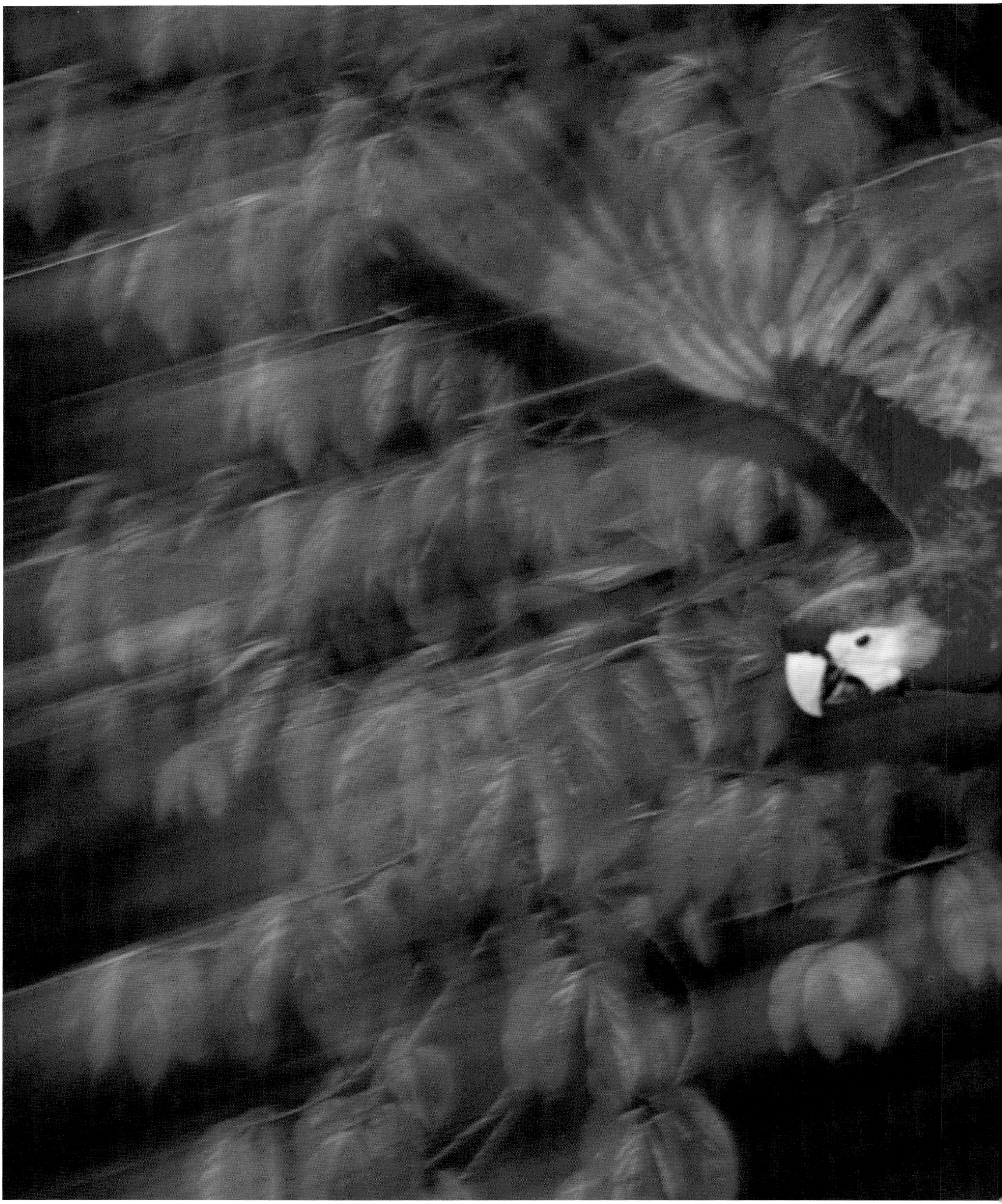

On wings that may span three feet, a fledgling Scarlet Macaw flies over a Peruvian rain forest. *Frans Lanting, 1994.*

A juvenile Northern Goshawk revs up its wings, preparing to fly. *Michael S. Quinton, 1994.*

The largest breeding colony of Cape Gannets is on South Africa's Malgas, or "mad goose," Island. *Chris Johns, 1995.*

An ʻIʻiwi, once called a Scarlet Honeycreeper, perches on a raspberry cane on Hawaii's Big Island. *Chris Johns, 1995.*

Using a cypress knee as a vantage point, an Anhinga surveys a Florida swamp. *Phil Schermeister, 1995.*

THEN & NOW

GRAY CROWNED-CRANES

1995: In an editorial meeting about a decade ago, a *National Geographic* photo editor promoted a portrait of a Gray Crowned-Crane by saying, "If Audrey Hepburn were a bird, she'd be this one." The Gray Crowned-Crane truly is one of nature's more generous gestures, a bird far prettier and elegant than it need be. Its long, feathery neck culminates in a head with an arresting facial pattern and startling blue eyes. Also, it is one of those uncommon species whose female and male share the same attractive plumage. Gray Crowned-Cranes range from eastern to southern Africa. The bird is sacred to the culture of the African Great Lakes region's Tutsis, among others, and appears on Uganda's flag, but poaching and encroachment on its wetland nesting habitat threaten its future. *(Michael Nichols)*

2015: As this studio close-up reveals, the Gray Crowned-Crane's striking head presents a study in textures. A large, white cheek patch, smoothly devoid of feathers, partially outlines an intense blue eye and contrasts with the rougher-hewn grayish black beak. The bird's forehead sports a knob of short, bristly feathers, as dense as a scrub brush, that yields to a red patch between it and the longer, stiff golden feathers of the crown, which are tipped in black. In the breeding season, Gray Crowned-Cranes of both sexes dance, bow, and jump (a lot), exuberant behavior that may burst forth at other times of the year as well. The species rests by roosting in trees, thanks to a grasping foot that is probably a vestigial feature from crane ancestors that other modern crane species have lost. *(David Liittschwager)*

A peacock spreads his magnificent tail to attract a mate. *Michael Melford, 1996.*

NEIGHBORLY PUFFINS

On land, puffins in the same area of a colony take time to socialize in small groups. Rocks and tussocks are the clubhouses where adults and immatures alike meet to impress potential mates or, it seems, just hang out on neutral ground. Older puffins struck me as being better acquainted with one another than most people are with their neighbors. Puffins ashore are always watching one another or poking a beak into another bird's business. There is nothing more fascinating to a puffin than another puffin. This inquisitiveness and sociability may look amusing, but it has a serious purpose: to synchronize activities in different parts of the colony and thus discourage predation. By boosting the chance of an individual's survival, curiosity about the puffin next door may have played a part in the evolution of the large breeding colony—a hallmark of puffin society.

—Kenneth Taylor

"Puffins," *National Geographic,* January 1996

An adult Atlantic Puffin acquires a billful of small fish to feed its chick on Scotland's Outer Hebrides. *Frans Lanting, 1996.*

TOP: A close-up highlights a Snowy Owl's yellow, catlike eyes. *Jim Brandenburg, 1996.*
BOTTOM: A Galápagos Hawk alights on a snag on Isabela Island. *Tui De Roy, 1997.*

Caught in reflection, Trumpeter Swans nap in a pond in Yellowstone National Park. *Michael S. Quinton, 1997.*

A Galápagos Penguin forages in shallow coastal waters off Bartolomé Island. *Tui De Roy, 1997.*

American Black Ducks and Mallards plow through algae on a Minnesota lake. *Jim Brandenburg, 1997.*

Sunrise greets a pair of Common Loons on Minnesota's Moose Lake. *Jim Brandenburg, 1997.*

Scarlet and Glossy Ibises rise from Venezuela's Orinoco Basin, where thousands congregate during the wet season. *Robert Caputo, 1998.*

A King Vulture pauses at the entrance to his nest in the Peruvian Amazon. *Tui De Roy, 1998.*

Domestic geese huddle on a bed of straw in Lüneberg, Germany. *Sisse Brimberg, 1998.*

A male Resplendent Quetzal peers out from his nest in a tree hollow in Guatemala. *Steve Winter, 1998.*

HORNBILL DELIVERY

The distinctive *kok* of a great pied hornbill interrupts our drowse. Coming closer, he thrashes the air with wings spanning five feet, making the chug-chug sound of a steam locomotive leaving a station. The bird alights on a branch near the nest, checks out the neighborhood, then flattens against the tree like a telephone lineman, holding fast with claws and propped by spread tail feathers. A dark body accentuates the glorious yellow of his bill and casque, shining in the sun. Pilai has explained that each day the bird applies a gloss of yellow oil from a preen gland at the base of his tail. He regurgitates a fig, dipping his enormous bill perpendicular so gravity can prompt the fig to roll down the inside of his beak like a returning bowling ball. He catches the fig precisely between the tips of his bill and delivers it to his mate through the slit . . . A female likes variety in her diet. "If a mate keeps bringing the same food," Pilai tells me, "she may throw it back at him."

—Michael E. Long

"The Shrinking World of Hornbills," *National Geographic,* July 1999

At a nest hole, a male Great Hornbill prepares to pass off food stored in his throat to feed his offspring. *Tim Laman, 1999.*

Following a centuries-old tradition, a Kazakh hunter works with his Golden Eagle. *David Edwards, 1999.*

OF A FEATHER

BIRDS AT HOME

BIRDS BECOME HOMESTEADERS for breeding purposes. Their nests can be as simple as a scrape in the sand or a few dried stems strewn on the ground, or as elaborate as an intricately woven basket or a beak-built mud cup a human potter might envy. Many species seek nest locations in trees or other vegetation, sometimes vying for space with squirrels, raccoons, or other birds. A good tree hollow is prime real estate for a young bird family, offering a lot of security for very little work. Some birds fashion their nests in or on buildings, while birds that nest colonially often skimp on structure, counting on safety in numbers.

TOP: A Willet nest with eggs sits in the middle of a fortress of tall grasses in coastal Virginia. *George Shiras 3d, 1906.*
OPPOSITE: A White Stork stands on its nest—a sign of good luck—on a building in Iraq. *Eric Keast Burke, 1922.*

TOP: An Elf Owl peers from its nest hole in an Arizona saguaro. *Lewis W. Walker, 1945.*

BOTTOM: A Chipping Sparrow squawks at a copperhead moving in on the eggs in its low-to-the-ground nest. *Walter A. Weber, 1954.*

OPPOSITE: A male Yellow Warbler takes a turn guarding his offspring in the nest likely built by his mate. *Frederick Kent Truslow, 1962.*

TOP: Gulls sit on nests built at intervals atop pilings in Oregon's Nehalem River. *Phil Schermeister, 1994.*
RIGHT: A Thick-billed Weaver clings to a papyrus stem, one of two sturdy anchors for its woven nest. *Mitsuaki Iwago, 1996.*

TOP: A masked weaver clings to his green-grass nest, shrieking and fluttering to attract a female. *Anup Shah, 2003.*

BOTTOM: Cliff Swallows scoop mud in their bills and carry it to their colony's chosen site to mold a nest. *Frans Lanting, 2008.*

OPPOSITE TOP: Flamingo parents cooperate in scraping together nest mounds. *Klaus Nigge, 2012.*

OPPOSITE BOTTOM: A European Starling visits its nestlings in a Colorado aspen. *Robbie George, 2012.*

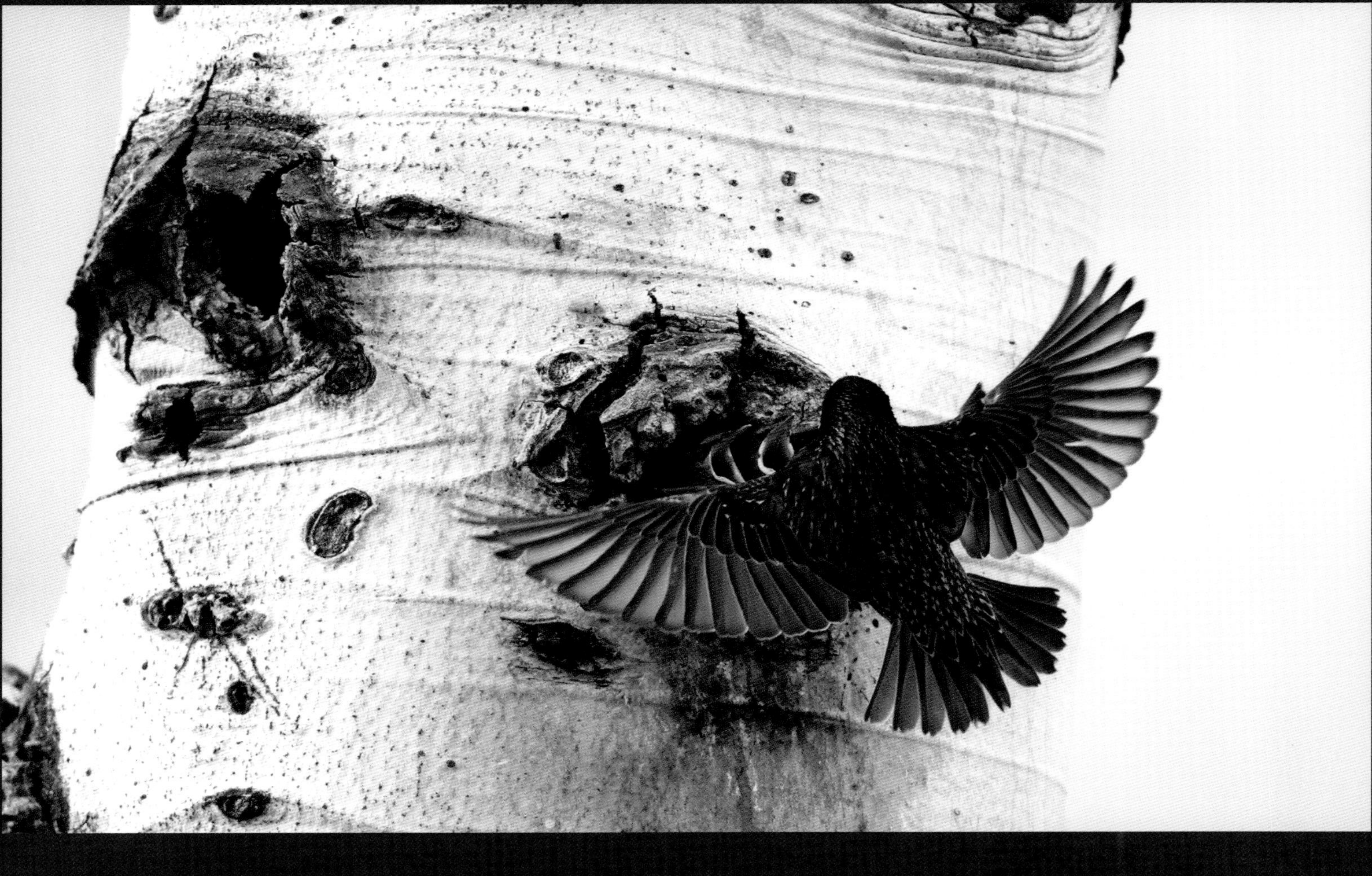

OPPOSITE: A Northern Flicker hides his chicks in the depths of a hollow tree. *Michael S. Quinton, 2014.*
TOP: A female Eclectus Parrot peeks out of a nest hole in Australia. *Michael Melford, 2014.*
BOTTOM: A jacana incubates an egg on a lily pad nest in Botswana. *Jason Edwards, 2014.*

CHAPTER FOUR

2000

2018

A male of the world's smallest bird species, the Bee Hummingbird, perches on a Cuban three-peso coin. *Anand Varma, 2015.*

FOR THE FUTURE

By the dawn of the new millennium, camera technology had become at once more sophisticated, affordable, and adaptable, thanks to digital photography, with its limitless exposures, immediate feedback, and greater possibilities for manipulation. Digital lightened photographers' loads and made light conditions less of an issue. Drones and satellite tracking presented new tools for searching out wildlife as well as advancing the cause of wildlife research—enhancing, for example, our understanding of the dynamics, magnitude, and sheer awesomeness of bird migrations. With ecological awareness and a commitment to preserving biodiversity as mandates, National Geographic remained focused on photojournalism with a cause. In March 2000, the magazine sent a team on assignment into Madidi National Park, a Bolivian national treasure of almost 4.5 million acres, regarded as one of the planet's most biodiverse locations. Guided by indigenous environmental activist Rosa María Ruiz, the team crossed this pristine rain forest, then under threat from a proposed hydroelectric dam project. The story was published with beautiful images of many of the park's more than one thousand bird species, which photographer Joel Sartore had captured at the cost of picking up a flesh-eating parasite (*pages 346–7*). Partly as a result of the international response to the article, the plan to build the dam was postponed, although Madidi activists today continue to fight similar proposals.

Penguin mania reached new heights in 2005, when the feature film *March of the Penguins* was released. Co-produced by National Geographic, it won a 2006 Academy Award for Best Documentary and grossed $127 million internationally. The film presents unblinkingly the bleak and beautiful Antarctic world of the Emperor Penguin and the ordeal of chick rearing in Earth's wind-battered deep freeze. As thoughtful viewers realized, director Luc Jacquet, the cinematographers, and other film crew endured the same daunting conditions as the penguins during the year-long filming.

Some 5,000 miles and multiple ecosystems away, photographer Tim Laman focused his lenses on two of the planet's flashiest bird groups, the bowerbirds and birds-of-paradise of New Guinea and Australia, avian Romeos who use colorful baubles and geometric dance moves to win their mates. Laman and collaborator Edwin Scholes, an ornithologist with the Cornell Lab of Ornithology, set a daunting task for themselves: to document all 39 species of New Guinea's elusive birds-of-paradise. It took 18 months of grueling work over a span of eight years, but they met their goal, acquiring a wealth of valuable observations and gorgeous images that illuminate the highly complex social lives birds often lead. The results of their efforts appeared in *Birds of Paradise: Revealing the World's Most Extraordinary Birds,* published by National Geographic in 2012.

PREVIOUS PAGES: A Trumpeter Swan finds refuge in Grand Teton National Park. *Robbie George, 2012.*

It is the rare article that stirs as great a response as did the 2013 story on songbird slaughter written by novelist and bird lover Jonathan Franzen. Franzen traveled to the Mediterranean to investigate the epidemic of birds killed for profit and sport. Photographer David Guttenfelder, a seasoned conflict reporter, noted that covering this mass killing of birds was like covering a war. Guttenfelder's haunting pictures of songbirds pinned in traps stirred powerful emotions, and the magazine received hundreds of letters from readers asking how they could help. The conversation continued long after the article appeared in print and was partially responsible for a two-year ban on songbird hunting in Albania, a key migration stopover point where the situation was most critical.

Art maintains its long legacy at National Geographic, but new mediums offer fresh possibilities for visual storytelling. Under former art director Juan Velasco, paintings and drawings increasingly appeared alongside digital art in the form of infographics, charts, animations, and maps to offer an arresting new way for pictures to tell a story and communicate complex scientific information. Transforming data into art requires both technical mastery and a creative eye, a special blend seen in the work of National Geographic graphic artists and cartographers. Senior graphics editor Fernando G. Baptista draws his art by hand or builds a physical model before translating his work to the computer, a technique he used to create several illustrated maps on bird migration (*page 255*).

Over time, photography as witness has surpassed the power of words in an image-driven global culture. It has also become a 24/7 medium, no longer contained by specific assignments and publication schedules. The National Geographic Instagram account, @NatGeo, gives posting privileges to professional photographers who upload regularly, inviting followers on assignment for an unfiltered view into their personal projects and expeditions. The account's diverse global audience—86 million followers and growing—is particularly receptive to animal content, and birds make for popular posts.

Yet wildlife photography has passed out of the strictly professional realm and into the hands of anyone with a good eye and a modest digital camera or a smartphone. This trend is reflected in Your Shot, a crowdsourced, curated site where the work of amateur shutterbugs is reviewed by National Geographic photographers and producers. The best submissions get published on the National Geographic website or in the magazines. More than 900,000 individuals participate, representing every country in the world. Indeed, photography is rapidly becoming one of the primary ways people interact with nature, and an excellent vehicle for inspiring a new generation of conservationists. As they train their camera's eye on a songbird at a feeder or geese flapping overhead, they open the door to a connection with the larger web of life. It is no wonder that many birdwatchers readily take up photography—both hobbies require self-discipline, passion, and a careful eye for detail.

When a family medical crisis in 2005 forced field photographer Joel Sartore to stay closer to his Nebraska home, he began visiting zoos and other captive-wildlife facilities to document animals, some on the brink of being lost to nature forever. He dubbed his ambitious project the Photo Ark, and by the beginning of 2018 he had photographed more than 7,500 of those species, including almost 2,000 birds. Sartore's style, along with that of other contemporary photographers such as Robert Clark (*page 384*), takes portraiture to a whole new level, allowing the viewer to savor every detail of an animal's appearance but also exposing, through the depths of the subjects' gazes, the complexity of life as experienced by nonhuman animals. By offering face-to-face contact, the portraits create a personal and intimate connection to the creatures that share our fragile planet—and present an eloquent, unspoken challenge for us to do the right thing (*page 477*).

As National Geographic expands its vast digital reach and worldwide audience, assignment photography and visual storytelling are more important than ever. Today's globetrotting shooters are versatile and tend to have an ease with technology that allows them to routinely customize equipment for special needs. A prime example is English photographer Charlie Hamilton James. For a 2016 *National Geographic* article, James was embedded in Yellowstone National Park, where he captured startling images of birds (*page 427*). Able to check his photos regularly on his laptop, James typifies the wildlife photographers of today, many of whom have never had the nail-biting experience of mailing precious rolls of exposed film back to headquarters, with fingers crossed until they arrive and breath held until the quality of the processed images is pronounced by the photo editor. Photographer Anand Varma, who has collaborated with a number of eminent scientists in the field, the lab, and the studio, uses sophisticated equipment and creative photographic setups to reveal what is invisible to the naked eye. His images of lightning-fast hummingbirds in action helped answer researchers' burning questions about their aerodynamics in flight and how their forked tongue sips nectar (*pages 468–9*).

We live in an age when everything old can be new again. A few years back, curator Sonia Voss visited the National Geographic archive in Washington, D.C., to view the work of pioneering wildlife photographer George Shiras 3d. Shiras had donated 2,400 of his glass plate negatives to the Society in 1928, in gratitude for the wide exposure the magazine had given his work beginning in 1906. Voss worked with the archive staff to have a selection of plates scanned and prepared for publication in a book and for a 2016 exhibit at the Musée de la Chasse et de la Nature (Museum of Hunting and Nature) in Paris. It was an apt venue, one that Shiras would have loved. The hunter who promoted bagging game with a camera instead of a gun and who used his platform as a former congressman to advocate successfully for the 1918 Migratory Bird Treaty Act was back in the news almost a hundred years later—a fitting tribute to both Grandfather Flash and National Geographic.

Birds are the canary in the coal mine on a global scale, signaling that what is happening to them affects all of us, and the whole planet. By focusing our efforts on the well-being of birds, we also help ourselves. To that end, National Geographic stands committed to reporting the facts about climate change as well as supporting research to understand its mechanisms and consequences.

The researchers, field biologists, journalists, and photographers have taken us places we've never been to witness birds we could never see with our own eyes, but they have also renewed our acquaintance with the familiar, elevating in all their splendor the birds in our everyday lives. Over more than a century, as *The Splendor of Birds* reveals, National Geographic has gone all in when it comes to birds, from legislative involvement to identification of hotspots to collecting their portraits *just in case*—using words, photography, and art to champion their cause. ■

In tandem flight, a mated pair of Red-and-green Macaws travel through Bolivia's Madidi National Park. *Joel Sartore, 2000.*

A male Great Frigatebird inflates his dramatic red pouch to attract a female. *Tui De Roy, 2000.*

A Gila Woodpecker pecks at a dead cholla cactus in Arizona's Sonoran Desert. *John Cancalosi, 2000.*

Caught up in the moment, Blue-footed Boobies engage in a courtship dance. *Tui De Roy, 2000.*

Sleeping American Avocets cast rippled shadows on the water. *Jim Brandenburg, 2000.*

A Snowy Egret's wing feathers catch the light off Florida's Sanibel Island. *Jim Brandenburg, 2000.*

A Crested Auklet perches on coastal rocks in Alaska. *Yva Momatiuk and John Eastcott, 2001.*

TOP: A male Thick-billed Green-Pigeon blends in with the leaves of a fig tree. *Tim Laman, 2001.*
BOTTOM: Flamingos fly over a carpet of green in Mozambique. *Chris Johns, 2001.*

A cozy pair of Black-footed Albatrosses find shade from the Hawaiian sun. *Tui De Roy, 2001.*

A Chestnut Wattle-eye peers out of foliage in Gabon. *Carlton Ward, Jr., 2002.*

A White-tipped Sicklebill has a perfectly decurved beak for sipping the nectar of a heliconia flower. *Michael and Patricia Fogden, 2002.*

Snares Penguins amble through the forest to their inland colony in New Zealand. *Frans Lanting, 2002.*

PRAIRIE DANCERS

At sunrise I watched the Attwater's prairie-chickens transform from mottled grouse into ornaments that exalted the flat coastal plain of Texas. They struck a rigid pose, tail feathers held over their backs in spiky fans. Special neck feathers cocked up behind their heads like horns. On each side of the throat big patches of golden skin with magenta margins inflated like balloons, and extra gold flared over the eyes. Strutting about, the performers bowed while deep notes boomed from the resonant air sacs. *Oo-loo-woo. Oo-loo-woo.* They then boogied, each stamping his feet as though trying to drive them into the ground. You've seen this before—the tail fans, the thumping footwork—in Plains Indian dances, drawn from the courtship displays of male prairie-chickens gathered each spring on their booming grounds. Suddenly the males have transformed again. Where a dozen paraded a second ago, I can't find one. Flattened with heads stretched out on the sod, the birds seem to have melted into it. Why? A hawk just swept by.

—DOUGLAS H. CHADWICK

"Down to a Handful," *National Geographic,* March 2002

A male of the endangered Attwater's race of Greater Prairie-Chicken survives in a pocket of protected habitat on the Texas plains. *Joel Sartore, 2002.*

Reacting to a disturbance, Rosy Bee-eaters take flight from their sandy rookery in Gabon. *Michael Nichols, 2002.*

A variety of macaws and parrots gathers on a riverside cliff in Peru to eat clay, possibly to augment their plant-based diet. *Maria Stenzel, 2002.*

A Bronze-tailed Plumeleteer flits through a Costa Rican rain forest. *Michael and Patricia Fogden, 2002.*

THEN & NOW

RAPTOR CHALLENGE

1939: As apex predators, eagles have a wide choice of prey. They preside over open steppes and plateaus with sparse vegetative cover, their preferred hunting grounds, and display violent aggression toward fellow eagles that encroach on their territory. They usually hunt small animals, making up in quantity what their prey lacks in size. At times, though, these fierce hunters armed with strong, lethal talons go after larger game, including deer. Fawns are usually an easier target, but eagles can successfully hunt full-size deer, too. Challenged on a snowy cliff, this Himalayan musk deer has no easy escape route and no antlers to help ward off attack. But the male's upper canine teeth grow long and sharp, offering some advantage in a fight. Walter A. Weber's masterly painting presents a lot of dramatic tension—and a strong suggestion that the Golden Eagle's grip could instantly provoke a fatal fall. *(Walter A. Weber)*

2002: Every picture tells a story, and this photo, shot by Norbert Rosing on a beach in Newfoundland, is no exception. But the plot line isn't a traditional tale of predator versus prey. The Bald Eagle is issuing a squawked warning to an interloping black-furred animal that is just a really muddy red fox. The message: "This is my turf!" He is declaring possession of the spawning capelin strewn all over the beach *(out of sight in the image)*. The summer spawn of this type of smelt is a windfall for many animals, including whales, seabirds, and even humans. No wonder tempers can run high. This confrontation lasted half an hour, with traded threats, feints, and attacks, the advantage passing back and forth between mammal and bird. Eventually, the two gave up, acknowledging that there was enough bounty for both species to feast on. *(Norbert Rosing)*

The world's only flightless parrot, a nocturnal, ground-dwelling Kakapo of New Zealand, lets out a call. *Frans Lanting, 2002.*

A Saltmarsh Sparrow clings acrobatically to dry reeds in a marsh. *Tom Vezo, 2003.*

Orange-chinned Parakeets poke holes in balsa blossoms to drink nectar. *Mattias Klum, 2003.*

Landing in a snowstorm, a Red-crowned Crane in Japan lowers its long black legs. *Tim Laman, 2003.*

A Hyacinth Macaw munches on a palm nut in central Brazil's tropical savanna. *Pete Oxford, 2003.*

A Blue-moustached Barbet in Peru displays patchwork plumage. *Pete Oxford, 2003.*

Red-legged Kittiwakes swarm the High Bluffs of St. George Island in Alaska's Pribilof Islands. *Joel Sartore, 2003.*

THEN & NOW

BALTIMORE ORIOLES

1934: When the Allan Brooks painting of Baltimore Orioles appeared in the July 1934 issue of *National Geographic,* the accompanying caption revealed much about the attitudes of the times. Titled "A Summer Flame from the Tropics Is Dapper 'Lord Baltimore,'" the piece describes a male Baltimore Oriole, "[s]porting the colors of Maryland's founder," as he "surveys his domain and whistles cheerily, while his lady weaves a beautiful hanging home of strings and plant fibers." The clearly anthropomorphized orioles replicated idealized 1930s domestic arrangements. In reality, the female's efforts determine success in the current nesting year and the future. A tree with a proven nest is repopulated in succeeding years, if not by the same birds then by other orioles. Females are known to recycle materials from existing nests, and also to add artificial fibers such as yarn, twine, and fishing line. *(Allan Brooks)*

2004: A photograph helps illuminate some of the differences between bird art and photography. While artist Allan Brooks deployed plenty of leaves to make the tree in the painting on the facing page look verdant, he placed them in the background, giving an unimpeded view of the intricate nest under construction. The nest in the photo, though, is only partially visible among the leaves that surround it. Brooks's painted oriole pair shows features of their plumage to their best advantage, but the bird in the photo, while unmistakably a Baltimore Oriole, is not unquestionably male; the full extent of his wing pattern is not shown, and his tail is obscured. Even his solo presence at the nest seems to belie the more traditional division of labor depicted in the painting. But unquestionably, the mate he is sharing parental duties with has clearly woven a strong, secure receptacle in which to start a family. *(George Grall)*

A trio of Little Owl owlets peer from an old barn window. *Robert Reijnen, 2004.*

Like an old-school screen star in furs, a domestic Jacobin pigeon sports an elaborate feathered collar. *Robert Clark, 2004.*

Common Ostriches tramp across salt pans in Botswana. *Robert B. Haas, 2004.*

In Guyana, an adult Hoatzin takes its chick under its wing. *Flip de Nooyer, 2004.*

TOP: A group of Dovekies, or Little Auks, line up on a rock. *Rinie van Meurs, 2004.*
BOTTOM: Mute Swan cygnet siblings hunker down on a parent's back. *Flip de Nooyer, 2004.*

Unfurling its yellow-shafted wings, a Northern Flicker emerges from its nest in a snag. *Michael S. Quinton, 2004.*

A Great Spotted Woodpecker follows a trail of English ivy up a tree trunk. *Frits van Daalen, 2004.*

The Blue Tit often forages on birch trees for caterpillars for its nestlings. *Frits van Daalen, 2004.*

SILENT MOUNTAIN

When I first went looking for great gray owls in the Bridger Mountains near my home in Bozeman, Montana, I heard them *hoo-hooing* for days before I spotted one. Over several more summers I photographed what came to be a familiar group of birds hunting and raising young on the brushy slopes. A couple of seasons after I made this picture, I went back. The big trees were all gone, cut by a timber company. The owls were gone too; I didn't hear a single hoot. I know that natural and man-made disturbances open up vital hunting space for great grays. But along with good perches and plenty of rodents, these birds need big trees for nest sites. I was stunned, and sad. I wondered how far the owls had traveled to find new homes, and whether I'd ever see them on this mountain again.

—DANIEL J. COX
"Great Gray Owls: Winged Silence,"
National Geographic, February 2005

A Great Gray Owl brings back a chipmunk meal to the family nest. *Daniel J. Cox, 2005.*

Unfurled crest feathers create a crown on a male Amazonian Royal Flycatcher in Guyana. *Wil Meinderts, 2005.*

TOP: Two American Crows appear in striking silhouette on a railing. *Al Petteway and Amy White, 2005.*

BOTTOM: The Black Skimmer's narrow bill, useful for fishing in skimming flight, is nearly unnoticeable face-on. *Klaus Nigge, 2005.*

A Red-legged Seriema in Brazil puts on a fierce threat display. *Pete Oxford, 2005.*

Intrepid Chinstrap Penguins huddle on a blue iceberg in stormy Antarctic seas. *Maria Stenzel, 2006.*

THE BIRDER'S CALL

What is it about birding that generates so much interest? Many of us are drawn to birding out of an appreciation of the beauty of birds and their variety of songs. The sight of a dozen or more species of warblers on a spring migration day, all with their own spectacular colors and distinctive patterns, is unforgettable. The long migratory journeys that certain species undertake—many thousands of miles, for some—and the mystery of how they reach their breeding and wintering grounds with such precision is awe-inspiring. There is also the excitement of the "treasure hunt": What is out there today? What will I find? Every outing offers the chance of finding and identifying a rare bird, a species very unusual for your area or even for North America as a whole. For those of us who have lived through a long winter with few birds among the bare branches, there is a thrill of anticipation when we see the greening of the forest, the budding of vegetation, and the arrival of the first spring migrants.

—JONATHAN ALDERFER AND JON L. DUNN
Birding Essentials (National Geographic, 2007)

A male Yellow Warbler croons from a maple branch in Maryland. *George Grall, 2012.*

TOP: An Ivory Gull comes in for a landing on a hunk of sea ice in the Canadian Arctic. *Paul Nicklen, 2007.*
BOTTOM: In Rome, a Peregrine Falcon chases a swarming flock of starlings. *Manuel Presti, 2007.*

A Grey-headed Albatross protects its chick from an incoming skua in New Zealand. *Frans Lanting, 2007.*

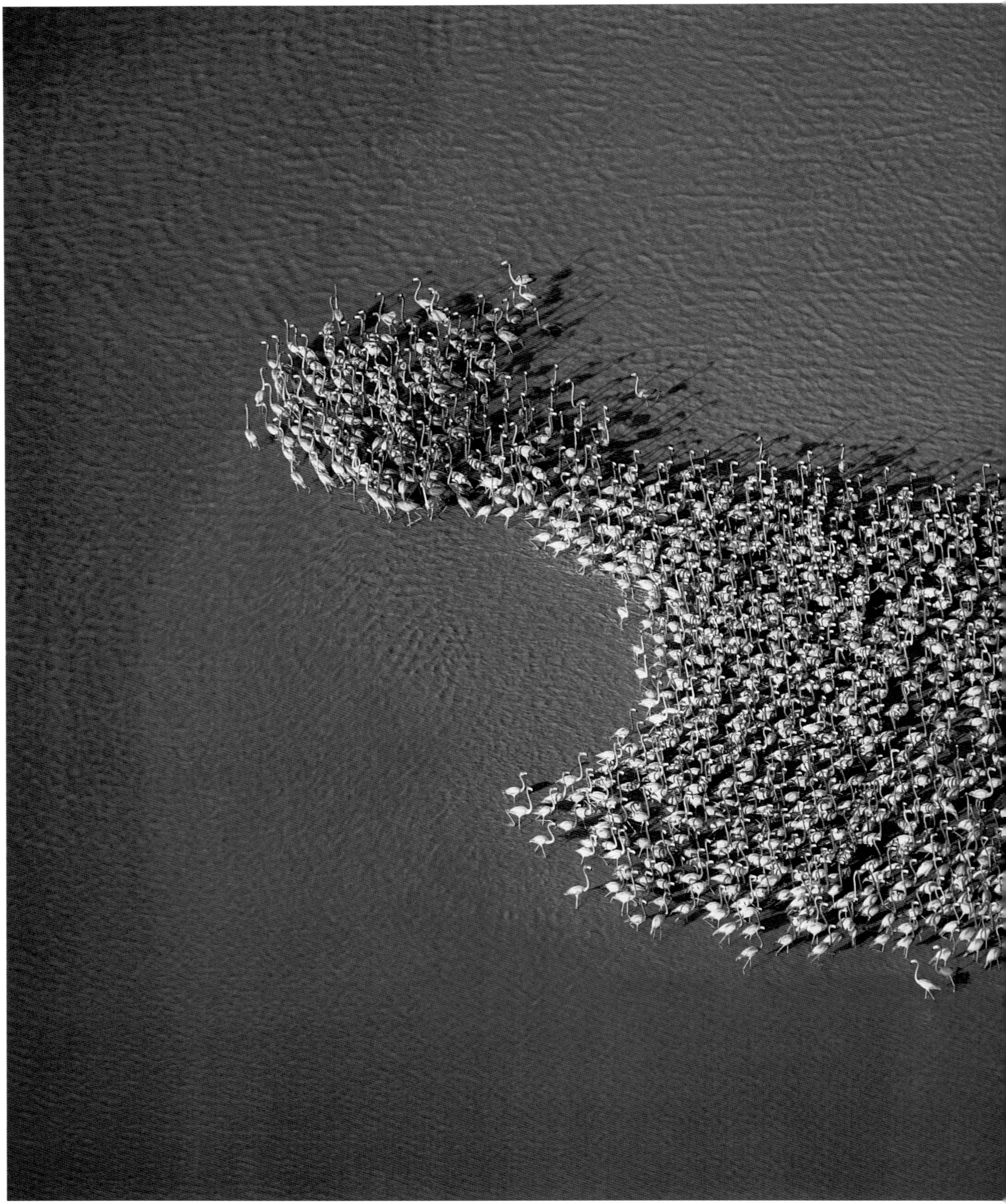

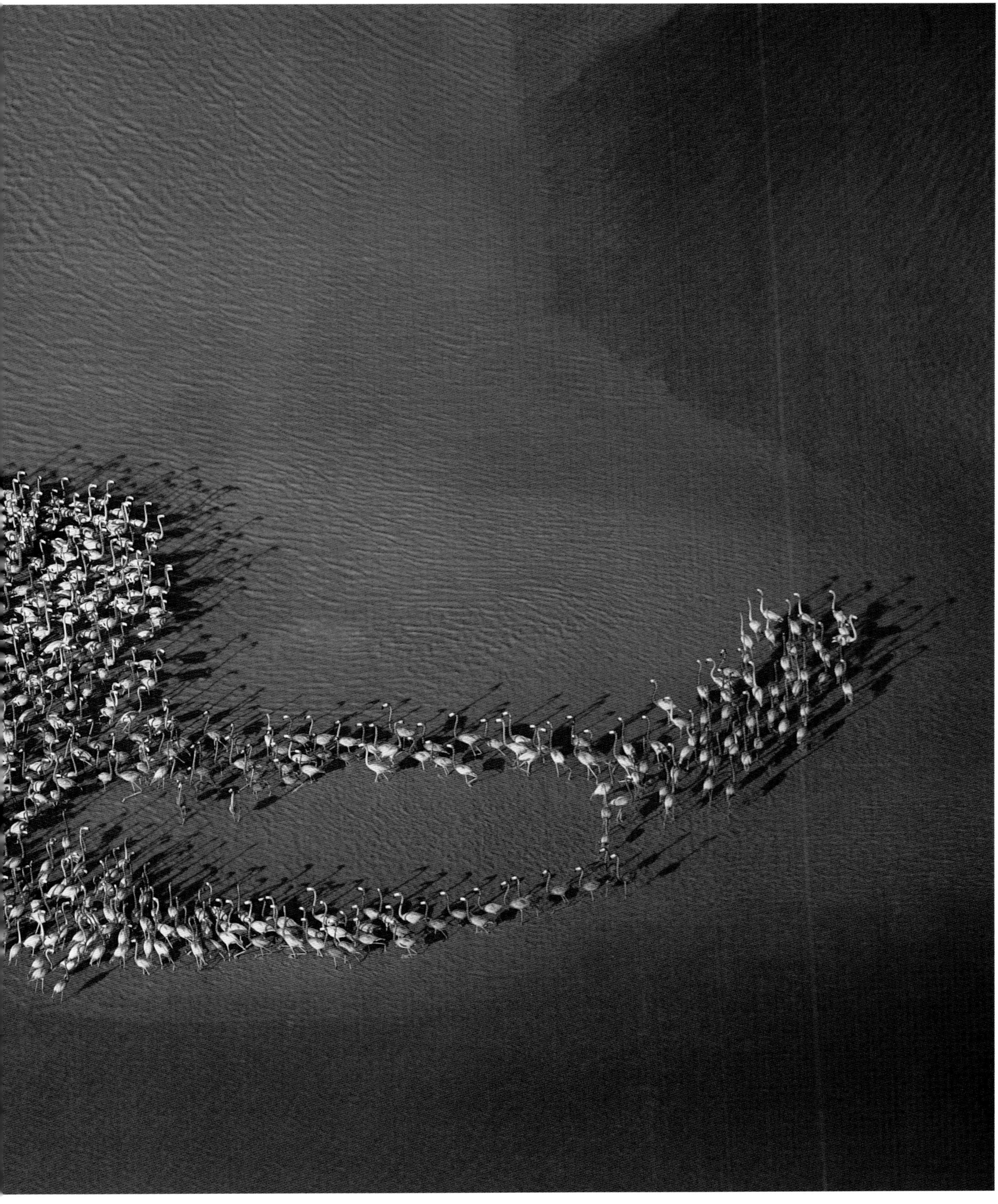

Flamingos serendipitously form a flamingo shape in a Gulf of Mexico lagoon. *Robert B. Haas, 2007.*

1971: What could more charismatic than a short, squat penguin waddling alone across an Antarctic snowfield? A short, squat penguin wearing a bright yellow backpack vest with a radio antenna waving above it, of course. When photographer Bill Curtsinger captured this scene, little did he know that he was laying claim to one of the most iconic images ever published in *National Geographic*. The shot made the magazine's cover in November 1971 and would go on to become one of the Society's most reproduced images. The Gentoo Penguin that was its subject was enrolled in a kind of "citizen science" program that monitored physiology and adaptation in the harsh Antarctic environment. The backpack contained equipment for tracking blood flow and pressure, both tested by a remotely triggered blood draw. Duties completed, the now famous Gentoo retired to a rookery. *(Bill Curtsinger)*

2007: Already proved to be reliable research assistants, penguins would later be tapped to test an updated version of the Crittercam, a device invented in 1986 by National Geographic's Greg Marshall. The wearable camera operates as a personal recorder, capturing video, audio, and environmental data on where an animal goes and what it sees. At about 80 pounds, Rodney the Emperor Penguin was one of the smallest animals to wear the 2.4-pound camera. Underwater, the device felt weightless and didn't cramp Rodney's style. He just continued with his daily routine, diving to 120 feet beneath the Antarctic ice before rocketing straight up

A California Scrub-Jay casts a knowing eye over the landscape. *Tim Fitzharris, 2007.*

Young Pileated Woodpeckers peer tentatively from their nest hole. *George Grall, 2007.*

Hawks overhead send Mallards into a frenzied escape from a South Dakota pond. *Laura Crawford Williams, 2007.*

White Eared Pheasants in China travel together. *Mark Moffett, 2008.*

A steely gaze contributes to this Martial Eagle's commanding presence. *Michael Nichols, 2008.*

Brown Pelicans display as they swap nest duties in the Galápagos. *Tui De Roy, 2008.*

A male Common Kingfisher displays perfect form, and a mirror image, in his dive. *Joe Petersburger, 2008.*

A colorful male European Bee-eater disables its meal before consuming it. *Joe Petersburger, 2008.*

A tagged "Northern" Spotted Owl maneuvers through California redwoods. *Michael Nichols, 2009.*

A Cape Barren Goose forages with her downy young in Australia. *Mitsuaki Iwago, 2009.*

Under a threatening sky, a male Eurasian Thick-knee, or stone-curlew, minds the nest. *Duncan Usher, 2009.*

Dovekies, a seabird species known in the British Isles as Little Auks, return from the sea to nest in Norway. *Paul Nicklen, 2009.*

TOP: An elegant Whooper Swan tucks into its wings to rest. *Stefano Unterthiner, 2010.*
BOTTOM: A Bald Eagle cools off in a plastic pool. *Melinda Dick, 2010.*

Whooping Cranes are the tallest birds in North America. *Klaus Nigge, 2010.*

THEN & NOW

BIRD SELFIES

1913: Pioneering explorer, congressman, writer, and photographer George Shiras 3d carried the fledgling pursuit of wildlife photography into the 20th century. He captured images at night using "flashlight" and pioneered many of the early techniques of remote imaging. He was also a patient man, willing to sit silently for endless hours in cramped, uncomfortable blinds. He had been watching the Black and Turkey vultures that circled his Florida cottage, hoping to get a shot from his hiding spot. After a "futile hour," he set up an automatic camera covered with palmetto leaves and rigged it to a string tied to a hunk of meat. He later returned to find "the bait was gone and the pulling string in a hopeless mess." Developing the plate from his camera, Shiras revealed the prize: the image of a calm quintet of vultures feeding on a windfall as decorously as dowagers at tea. *(George Shiras 3d)*

2016: Fast-forward a hundred years: Remote imaging has gone high-tech, but patience and luck still figure into the process. National Geographic photographer Charlie Hamilton James reported that it took about 200,000 tries to obtain this image from Grand Teton National Park of a grizzly chasing off marauding ravens at a carcass dump. (Park rangers there remove roadkill to areas safely away from tourists.) James was monitoring the site weekly, with the help of armed rangers to protect him on his sprints to and from the camouflaged camera box. He would retrieve the memory cards, scroll through the images on his laptop, and then replace the cards in the camera. After five months of this drill, the kind of image he had hoped for popped up on the screen. A charging grizzly had tripped the Nikon's motion sensor, perfectly capturing the commotion in progress. *(Charlie Hamilton James)*

A young Steller's Sea-Eagle stalks through the snow on Russia's Kamchatka Peninsula. *Sergey Gorshkov, 2010.*

A Sooty Albatross nests on a steep cliff on a South Atlantic island. *Tui De Roy, 2010.*

Vieillot's Black Weavers in Uganda tend to their intricately woven nests. *Joel Sartore, 2010.*

A pheasant's down is similar to filaments that covered the pterosaurs, extinct flying reptiles. *Robert Clark, 2011.*

Imperial Shags boast deep blue eyes and orange bill knobs. *Ralph Lee Hopkins, 2011.*

TOP: Hens of Silkie Showgirl, a domestic breed of chicken, live at the Fort Worth Zoo. *Joel Sartore, 2011.*
BOTTOM: Experimental size-based breeding produced an eight-week-old chick that dwarfs its age mate. *Vincent J. Musi, 2011.*

An adult Emperor Penguin creates a colorful contrast in a mob of fuzzy chicks. *Frans Lanting, 2011.*

A Piping Plover offers cover to its chicks on a chilly Massachusetts beach. *Michael Milicia, 2012.*

American Flamingos get their coral hue from the brine shrimp they eat. *Klaus Nigge, 2012.*

A Black-headed Weaver, foreground, seems to be beckoning a waiter to a safari lodge lunch table in Uganda. *Joel Sartore, 2012.*

Vision in white: A leucistic peacock lacks pigmented plumage but still shows pigment in its eyes. *Joe Petersburger, 2012.*

A small but fierce Merlin applies lethal force to a Common Snipe on moorland in Northern England. *Steve Mills, 2012.*

THEN & NOW

CAPTURING CASSOWARIES

1908: Early 20th-century scientists and ethnographers found a fertile field for exploration in New Guinea. Its landscapes, people, and flora and fauna, including birds, offered limitless novelty. Few birds intrigued like the Southern Cassowary, an enormous, flightless species next in mass in the avian world only to the two species of ostrich. Females, bigger than males, can reach six feet tall and weigh up to 160 pounds. Adults sport large casques (hollow, hornlike growths) on their crowns that may be sexual adornments. Their body plumage consists of a mop of shaggy black feathers. New Guinea tribes hunt and also raise the cassowary for food and have made use of almost every part of its body down to the sharp toenails, used for arrow points. Young cassowaries, such as the one depicted in the photo, are captured by being driven into nets stretched out in the forest. *(Thomas Barbour)*

2013: One of the three cassowary species, the Southern Cassowary is found in Australia, where it roams rain forests in North Queensland, sometimes wandering into gardens. If a cassowary becomes used to receiving human handouts, it may attack if expectations are not met. They are not birds to be taken lightly—a kick from an adult cassowary can break a leg or crack a skull. Left to their own devices, cassowaries are connoisseurs of rich, ripe fruits. A young cassowary learns about preferred fruits from its father, in the manner of this Queensland chick plucking a berry under dad's expert supervision. Males also incubate eggs and provide child care for as long as nine months. As a local human mother of five quipped to Olivia Judson, who wrote about "Big Bird" for the September 2013 *National Geographic*, "I'm coming back as a female cassowary." *(Christian Ziegler)*

Sandhill Cranes migrate over the Sangre de Cristo Mountains, in southern Colorado. *Keith Ladzinski, 2013.*

TOP: A Burrowing Owl stretches outside its burrow in South Dakota. *Michael Forsberg, 2014.*
BOTTOM: On an island off the coast of Wales, an Atlantic Puffin peers from its burrow. *Danny Green, 2014.*

A Southern Yellow-billed Hornbill preens its feathers in South Africa. *Bertie Gregory, 2014.*

A male Wood Duck rears out of the water on a North Carolina lake. *Robbie George, 2014.*

With a hatchling on its back and eggs underneath, a Great Crested Grebe multitasks. *Bertie Gregory, 2014.*

Spectacled Eiders appear to mug for the camera in a studio shot. *Joel Sartore, 2015.*

A high-speed camera captures a pigeon's sweeping wings mid-flight. *Roe Ethridge, 2015.*

Mist nets are used by conservationists and scientists to temporarily trap and release wild birds such as this Keel-billed Toucan. *Todd Forsgren, 2016.*

VILIFIED VULTURES

The vulture may be the most maligned bird on the planet, a living metaphor for greed and rapaciousness. Leviticus and Deuteronomy classify vultures as unclean, creatures to be held in abomination by the children of Israel. In his diary during the voyage of H.M.S. *Beagle* in 1835, Charles Darwin called the birds "disgusting," with bald heads "formed to wallow in putridity." Among their many adaptations to their feculent niche: the ability to vomit their entire stomach contents when threatened, the better to take quick flight. Revolting? Perhaps. But vultures are hardly without redeeming values. They don't (often) kill other animals, they probably form monogamous pairs, and we know they share parental care of chicks, and loaf and bathe in large, congenial groups. Most important, they perform a crucial but massively underrated ecosystem service: the rapid cleanup, and recycling, of dead animals.

—Elizabeth Royte

"Bloody Good," *National Geographic,* January 2016

A scrum of vultures feed on a carcass in Tanzania's Serengeti National Park. *Charlie Hamilton James, 2016.*

TOP: This Green-headed Tanager is a rain forest resident in Brazil. *Alex Saberi, 2016.*
BOTTOM: An Orange-eyed Thornbird perches in a Brazilian rain forest. *Alex Saberi, 2016.*

A water buffalo skull provides a perch for Red-and-yellow Barbets in Tanzania. *Annie Griffiths, 2016.*

CARMELA FRAIL
MITCHELL FRAIL

Rose-ringed Parakeets sail over the headstones in a London cemetery. *Sam Hobson, 2016.*

A Red-footed Booby's signature red webbed feet display claws. *Thomas P. Peschak, 2016.*

A Chestnut-colored Woodpecker feasts on fruit in Costa Rica. *George Grall, 2017.*

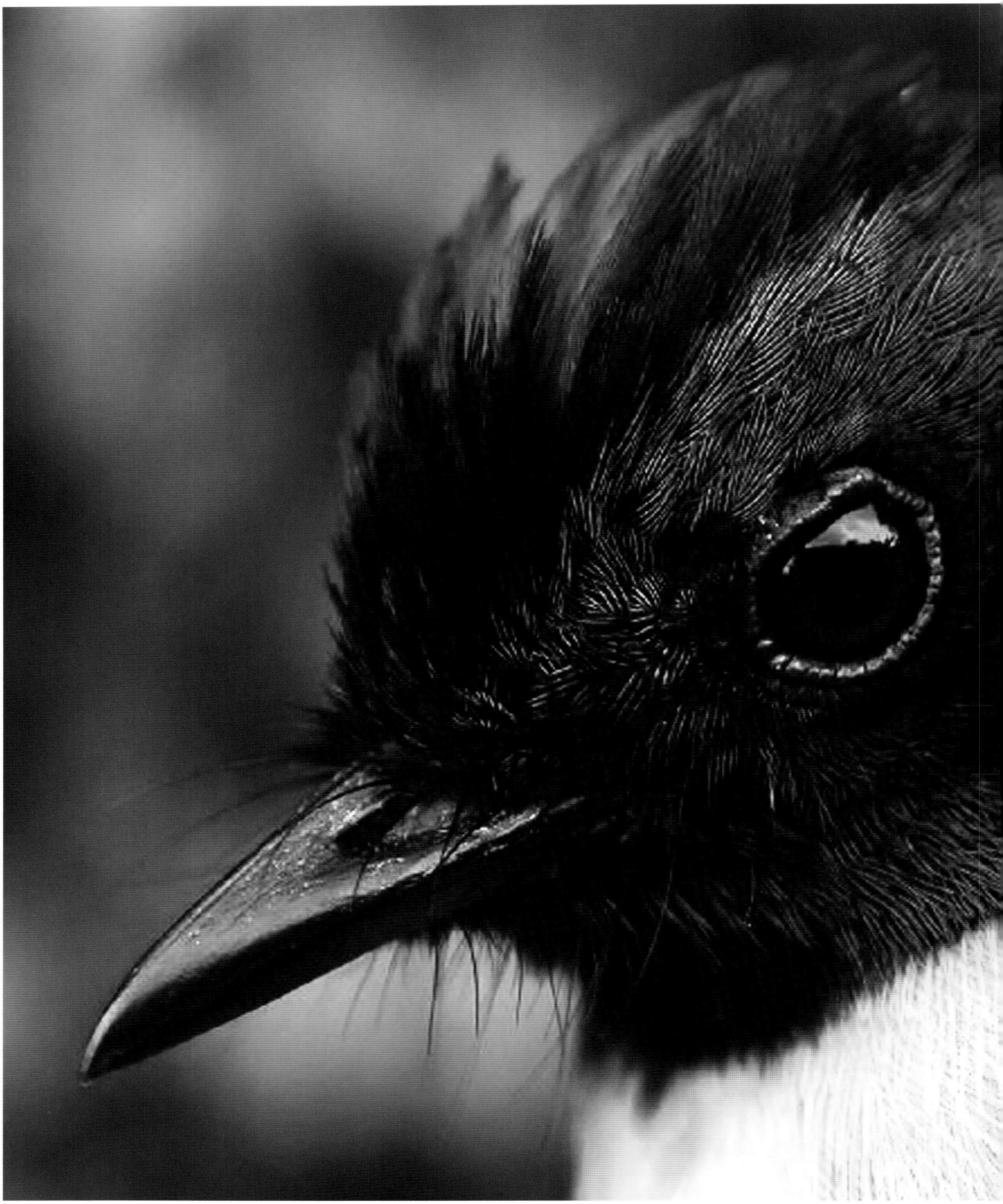

A Slate-throated Whitestart in Costa Rica sports a reddish crown. *Cagan H. Sekercioglu, 2017.*

A Burrowing Owl displays a prominent white "unibrow." *Kent Kobersteen, 2017.*

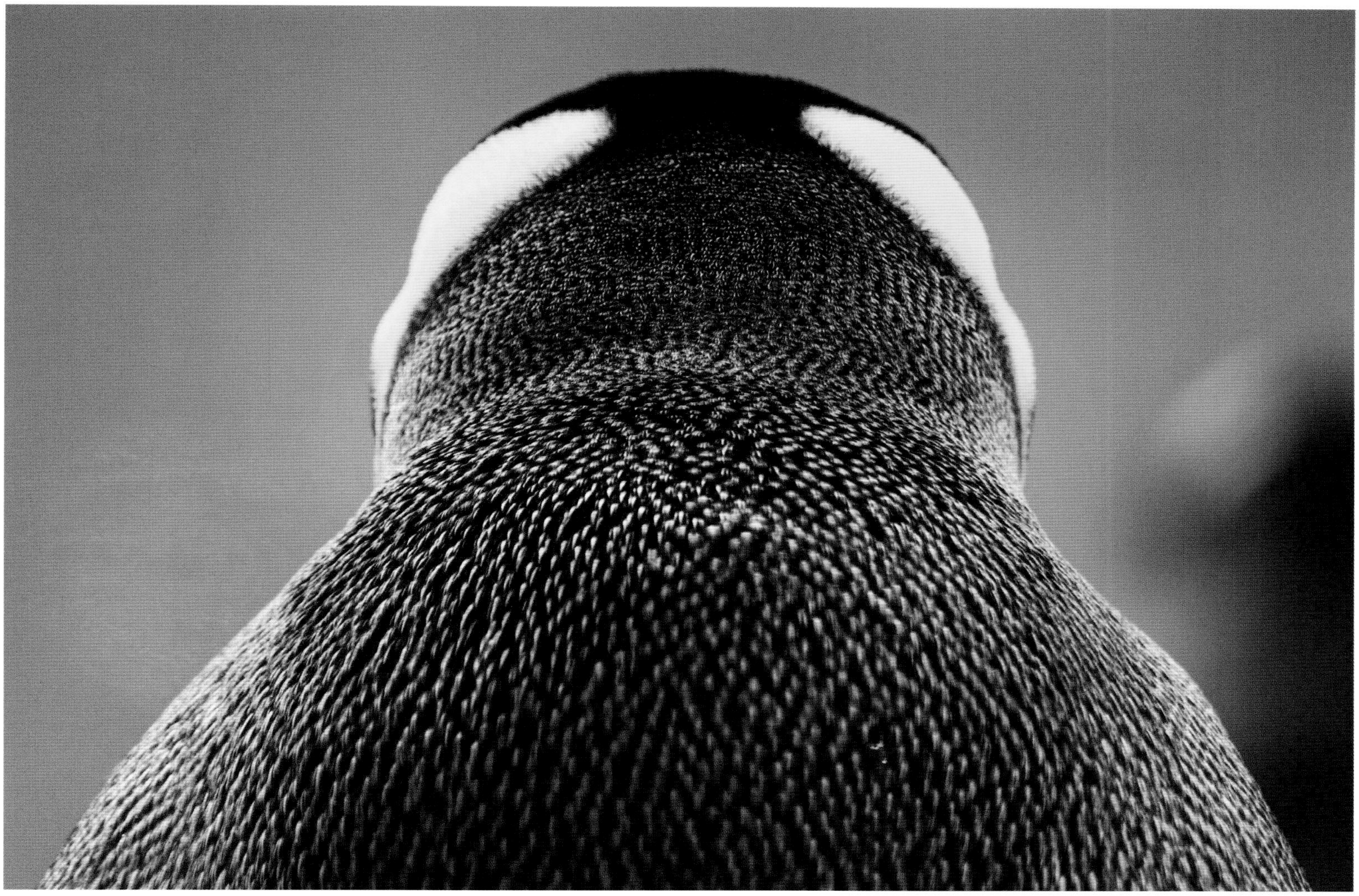

Bright yellow-orange head and neck feathers identify a King Penguin from the rear. *Jason Edwards, 2017.*

A nectar-filled glass vessel clearly displays an Anna's Hummingbird's forked tongue. *Anand Varma, 2017.*

A volcanic slope provides a landing place for a Galápagos Hawk. *Thomas P. Peschak, 2017.*

The Black-necked Stork in Australia has iridescent feathers on its head and neck. *Michael Melford, 2017.*

THEN & NOW

OSTRICH APPEAL

1942: As the world's largest bird, standing some 10 feet tall and weighing up to 400 pounds, a Common Ostrich can easily accommodate a rider. This young woman on an ostrich farm in Oudtshoorn, South Africa, the "ostrich capital of the world," handles her flightless avian mount. Riding an ostrich is a tricky business. With no reins for control, the rider can only hang onto the wings and hope for the best. The photographer also witnessed an ostrich "derby," in which the birds raced off in random directions at the starting signal. By the time of this photograph, the ostrich business in South Africa was in decline. The last surge in demand for ostrich plumes for women's hats had occurred just prior to World War I. By 1942, the export business had shifted to ostrich skin, popular for making shoes, handbags, and souvenirs. *(W. Robert Moore)*

2017: Germans are very fond of ostrich meat. In fact, they were the largest importers of the product from South Africa until a recent ban prohibited its export due to avian influenza. Germany has also created its own supply of the low-calorie, low-fat, low-cholesterol protein source, and is now home to some 150 commercial ostrich farms, or *Straussenfarmen,* where the birds are raised free range and fairly sustainably, which adds to their appeal. At the ostrich farm pictured here, one-week-old chicks mill about under adult supervision. Eggs are typically removed immediately after being laid. The last clutches of the year, however, are left with their mothers, to be incubated and the chicks cared for after hatching. Judging by the success of these farms, ostriches seem not to be affected by the colder German climate. *(Klaus Nigge)*

Bar-tailed Godwits forage in a New Zealand estuary. *Jonathan Harrod, 2018.*

LENS OF LEGACY

Whether these species survive into the future is really up to all of us, and that all starts with a simple introduction like the Photo Ark, showing these thousands of amazing species to many people who might never see them any other way. We won't save them if we don't know they exist. So when birds serenade us at sunrise, their ancient calls resonate far beyond attracting mates and defending territories. That's actually the voice of Wilderness you're hearing. They sing from the heart, resilient and determined. And the best part is they'll be around for generations to come . . . but only if given proper stewardship . . . Good stewardship takes effort, but it's so worth it. The future of birds, and us, are intertwined more than we know. We soar, or plummet, together.

—Joel Sartore
Birds of the Photo Ark (National Geographic, 2018)

A Blue-faced Honeyeater strikes a pose at the Houston Zoo. *Joel Sartore, 2018.*

A Northern Goshawk tucks in her wings and streaks through tree branches at a high speed. *Charlie Hamilton James, 2018.*

TOP: A captive raven quickly completes a test to capture meat on the end of a string. *Charlie Hamilton James, 2018.*

BOTTOM: Arnie, a European Starling, has a preference for the classical composers. *Charlie Hamilton James, 2018.*

A Tanimbar Corella at a research aviary displays the tool he made to retrieve a cashew. *Charlie Hamilton James, 2018.*

In a timeless scene, Sandhill Cranes gather along the Platte River in Nebraska. *Stephen Wilkes, 2018.*

OF A FEATHER

FOCUS ON FEATHERS

FEATHERS SET THE BIRD WORLD APART. We now know they adorned some familiar dinosaurs, having appeared in the fossil record. Wing feathers of today are precise in structure and arrangement, designed for flight, but they represent just one feature of a bird's total plumage. Feathers also provide insulation, camouflage, and adornment. Males display many spectacular feather colors and over-the-top shapes (such as intricate quills and crests) as part of their reproductive tool kit. Human cultures have long prized feathers to indicate status, make a fashion statement, and use in ceremony.

TOP: A Crow chief sits in feathered splendor on a Montana reservation. *Edwin L. Wisherd, 1927.*

OPPOSITE: The narrower falcon wing allows swift flight in the open; the wider goshawk wing lets the bird maneuver in cover. *Louis Agassiz Fuertes, 1920.*

TOP: An Araucana rooster boasts a fancy cape and whisker feathers. *B. Anthony Stewart, 1948.*
BOTTOM: The male Magnificent Riflebird flashes an iridescent neck in his energetic courtship dance. *Walter A. Weber, 1950.*
OPPOSITE: Close up, the brown, black, and white of pheasant feathers resemble pinecone scales. *Farrell Grehan, 1982.*

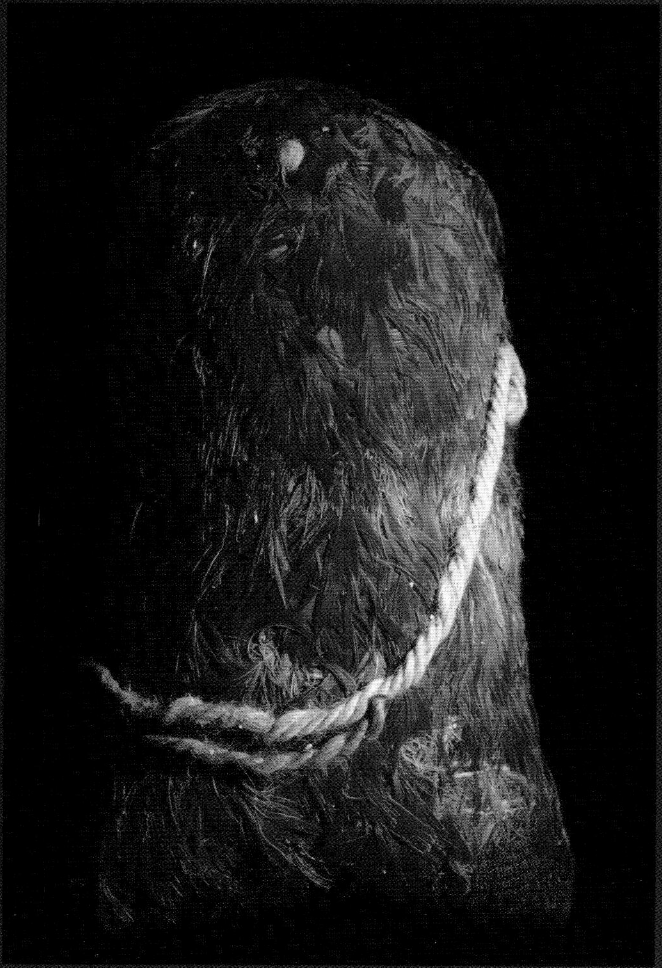

TOP: The fine feathers of an ʻIʻiwi match the delicacy of a mosquito's wing. *Chris Johns, 1995.*
BOTTOM: Feathers adorn a coca bag that was buried with Inca mummies in the High Andes. *Maria Stenzel, 1999.*
OPPOSITE TOP: The pattern of banded feathers endures in a bird fossil. *Jonathan Blair, 2000.*
OPPOSITE BOTTOM: A waterbird hunter wears an egret mask as cover in Pakistan's Indus River while a live heron he trapped earlier perches nearby. This style of hunting is depicted in artifacts dating to 3300 B.C. *Randy Olson, 2000.*

LEFT: The King of Saxony Bird-of-paradise sports long crown quills. *Tim Laman, 2007.*
TOP: Who's a pretty bird? The Sulphur-crested Cockatoo! *Robert Clark, 2008.*

OPPOSITE: The hues of a Scarlet Macaw wing present a rainbow progression. *Kevin Schafer, 2010.*
TOP: The tail disks of a King Bird-of-paradise bobble during courtship displays. *Frans Lanting, 2011.*
BOTTOM: The wisps and filaments of Red Bird-of-paradise flank feathers are important in courtship. *Robert Clark, 2011.*
NEXT PAGES: An Eastern Screech-Owl blends seamlessly into a woodpecker's nest hole. *Graham McGeorge, 2013.*

A vintage painting depicts a trio of ibis species. *Allan Brooks, 1932.*

CONTRIBUTORS

PHOTOGRAPHERS

Since first arriving as an intern in 1967, **SAM ABELL** has lent his magic touch to National Geographic photography. Found in numerous books and magazine articles, Abell's pictures illuminate such places as Newfoundland, Australia, Japan, and the American West and such people as the likes of Leo Tolstoy, Lewis Carroll, and Winslow Homer. His photographs are widely admired for their beauty, grace, and great contemplative power.

THOMAS J. ABERCROMBIE (1930–2006) was born in Stillwater, Minnesota, and attended St. Paul's Macalester College, majoring in art and journalism. He joined National Geographic as a photographer in 1955 and was promoted to its foreign editorial staff a year later. During his 38 years with the Society, Abercrombie photographed and wrote 43 articles for *National Geographic* magazine. He became the first correspondent to reach the geographic South Pole.

ARTHUR A. ALLEN's ▼ (1885–1964) professional life revolved around Cornell University. He obtained three degrees there, joined the faculty as the first U.S. professor of ornithology, and was founding director of the Cornell Lab of Ornithology. A pioneering photographer, Allen excelled at capturing images under all conditions—whether in the backyard or a remote swamp. His photos illustrate the 18 articles he authored over three decades for *National Geographic*.

Embracing photography at an early age, **JAMES L. AMOS** nevertheless took a roundabout way to practicing it. After graduating from the Rochester Institute of Technology, the Michigan native was for 16 years an Eastman Kodak technical representative. He was nearly 40 before he joined National Geographic—only to be named Magazine Photographer of the Year in both 1970 and '71. Before retiring in 1993 he had published more than 20 stories on various technological and regional American subjects.

SPENCER R. ATKINSON (1886–1970) was a skilled photographer yet also a pioneering orthodontist who collected the skulls of children to better understand anatomical changes during childhood. Much of the nature photography he pursued supported the writings of his wife, Agnes Akin Atkinson, who was known for her charming stories of the wild animals they befriended near their Pasadena, California, home, including several articles published in *National Geographic*.

When **THOMAS BARBOUR** (1884–1946) married in 1906, he took his wife on a long honeymoon to Asia. Traveling as far as China and New Guinea, the two photographed animals and collected specimens. Apart from his extensive travel, Barbour was pretty much a Harvard lifer, obtaining a bachelor's, master's, and doctoral degree there and joining the faculty as curator of reptiles and amphibians at the university's Museum of Comparative Zoology, before becoming the museum's director.

Australian **CHARLES L. BARRETT** (1879–1959) spent an idyllic childhood near Melbourne, immersed in nature and particularly fond of birds. He later joined the staff of the city's *Herald* newspaper, where he kept the public informed about natural history for the next 33 years. Despite a lack of formal training, Barrett was a founding member of the Royal Australasian Ornithologists Union and editor of its journal, *The Emu*.

It was in the 1950s that Australian couple **DES** (1927–2009) **AND JEN BARTLETT** ▲ began the remarkable career that soon made them among the most renowned wildlife photographers and filmmakers in the world. Along the way, they contributed to 11 stories in *National Geographic* (and an Emmy Award–winning film), their subjects ranging from Patagonia to Namibia.

Born in Halifax, Nova Scotia, **LOUISE BIRT BAYNES** (1876–1958) immigrated with her family to Boston, where she studied art. She was already well into her own photographic study of nature when she married noted naturalist Ernest H. Baynes in 1901. "Birt," as she was called, collaborated with her husband for the next 25 years, continuing the work that made her one of the early 20th century's pioneering women photographers.

JAMES P. BLAIR forged his photographic style through close exposure to such formative influences as Roy E. Stryker and Harry Callahan. For 32 years (1962–1993) as a National Geographic staff photographer, Blair undertook more than 40 assignments whose subjects ranged from computer chips to eclipses, but his most lasting work has focused on social or environmental themes and photojournalism—he won the 1977 Overseas Press Club Award for his striking coverage of apartheid in South Africa.

JONATHAN BLAIR was first captivated by photography while taking pictures of stars at Northwestern University's observatory. Later, while working as a park ranger, he had his photos of Yosemite published in *National Geographic* magazine. This kicked off four decades of freelance assignments that have taken Blair, a versatile photographer who leans toward underwater and archaeological stories, from Hawaii to the Mediterranean to the high Himalayas.

HERMAN T. BOHLMAN (1872–1943) became a local avian expert by tromping around the marshy areas of Portland, Oregon, with his childhood friend William L. Finley. He and Finley would show lantern slides to the public and also published photo essays about birds and wildlife in the *Oregonian*. Scientific data the two amassed from their observations helped support conservation efforts, which resulted in the designation of wildlife refuges.

Most of the life of **BEECHER S. BOWDISH** (1872–1963) revolved around birds. He observed them, photographed them, advocated for them, and even patented a device for feeding them. Bowdish shared his knowledge through frequent illustrated lectures and the publication of articles and photographs in books and in many popular and scientific journals of the day. He also served as the secretary of the New Jersey Audubon Society.

Experienced reporter **DAVID S. BOYER** joined National Geographic in 1952, after a stint as a U.S. Navy photographer. He was a writer and photographer for the magazine for 37 years, specializing in national parks and wilderness areas. Boyer also traveled from Jerusalem to Rome for an article about St. Paul. His famed, poignant image of young John F. Kennedy, Jr., saluting the casket bearing his slain father won numerous awards.

Though he has shot pictures everywhere from Africa to Japan for *National Geographic*, **JIM BRANDENBURG**'s career pivots on the prairies and woods of his native Minnesota. In 23 magazine features and several books, the world-renowned nature photographer has depicted wilderness subjects ranging from the white wolves of Ellesmere Island to a profile of conservationist Aldo Leopold. In 1999 he established the Brandenburg Prairie Foundation to promote awareness of that vanishing ecosystem.

STANLEY BREEDEN, who was born in the Netherlands, immigrated to Australia in his early teens. Over a long career, he has established himself as one of Australia's pioneering nature photographers and documentary filmmakers. In 1986 he won an Emmy for the National Geographic television special *Land of the Tiger*. Today, he and his wife, Kaisa, make highly detailed images using specialized digital photography techniques they themselves developed.

Born in Denmark, **SISSE BRIMBERG** managed her own photography studio in Copenhagen before moving to the United States to shoot on contract for National Geographic. Since that time, her work—whether on the Vikings, Catherine the Great, the Lascaux caves, or chocolate, among many assignments—has been published in more than 30 issues of the magazine. She and her husband, Cotton Coulson, founded Keenpress Photography, in Denmark.

LEVERETT W. BROWNELL (1871–1951) joined the Camera Club of New York at the age of 25 and soon began to share his photos of birds and other animals with the club's elite membership, including renowned photographer Alfred Stieglitz. In 1915, Brownell opened his own studio, in New Jersey, *and used it as a base for the enormous collection* of natural history photographs he created over his lifetime.

Photographer and journalist **ERIC KEAST BURKE** (1896–1974) was a New Zealand native who moved to Australia with his family as a young boy. As a soldier during World War I, he landed in Mesopotamia with an Allied Naval squadron, and while there, developed an abiding interest in architecture and archaeology in the cradle of civilization. Upon his return to Australia, he worked under his father at Kodak's *Australasian Photo-Review* and championed photography's role in Australian history.

Biologist **ALVIN R. CAHN** (1892–1971) came at nature photography from an academic perspective. He trained his keen observational eye on many species, publishing reports on a range of animals, from birds to mammals to turtles to fish. As a Naval Reserve officer called up during World War II, he was stationed in the Aleutians and was credited with identifying and saving archaeological treasures there from destruction.

Trained as a zoologist, **JOHN CANCALOSI** worked as a field biologist for state and federal agencies and as a conservation educator in several western states. A passion for travel and photography led to a career switch, and significant acclaim. Cancalosi's wildlife photographs have been published internationally, garnering many awards, including BBC Wildlife Photographer of the Year. He particularly enjoys documenting wildlife in Arizona's Sonoran Desert.

ROBERT CAPUTO began his long involvement with Africa when, traveling after college, he met filmmaker Hugo van Lawick in Tanzania and learned to shoot wildlife documentaries. This led him to the then-named New York University Film School, and then back to Africa, where he began freelancing for National Geographic in 1980. His articles have covered famine, war, and wildlife across the continent, while his journey up the Nile River resulted in both a book and a television documentary.

Born in Cheshire, England, **J. ALLAN CASH** (1902–1974) made his mark as a travel photographer. If Cash had a motto, it might have been "Have Leica, will travel." In the 1930s he embarked on a world tour with his trusty camera in hand, snapping shots of the birds of the British Isles, portraits in Africa and Asia, and scenes of London's bustling streets. After marrying a fellow photographer and travel *writer in 1939, Cash opened a commercial studio in* London with his wife, Betty; their archive included images from more than 90 countries.

LYNWOOD M. CHACE (1901–1994) of Massachusetts was an early practitioner of animal portraiture who created elaborate setups to achieve his unusual range of portraits. Fish were acquired in local ponds and brought to an aquarium in his studio. Lighting illuminated the tank, and the image was captured when the fish neared the glass wall. Chace also kept a pet Marabou Stork, which he taught to catch a ball.

PAUL CHESLEY, a native Minnesotan, began shooting for the Society in 1975, and he has now completed 35 Geographic projects. Though he has crossed Canada by train, hiked along the Continental Divide, and explored hidden corners all over North America for National Geographic's Book Division, Chesley has enjoyed most those assignments that took him to Asia and the Pacific Ocean.

Based in New York City, **ROBERT CLARK** ▲ is a freelance photographer known for his innovation and his ability to document the world in all its beauty and diversity. His images have appeared on more than a dozen *National Geographic* covers and in more than 40 of the magazine's articles. In one extensive visual study of the science of evolution, Clark photographed hundreds of feathers from birds of the world.

Photographer **HOWARD H. CLEAVES** (dates unknown) was an early adopter of the concept of shooting wildlife with a camera instead of a gun, supplying more than 45 images to the 1914 *National Geographic* article "Hunting with the Lens." Cleaves served as cinematographer for the 1929 Pinchot South Sea Expedition, which traveled to the Caribbean and South Pacific to collect specimens for the Smithsonian Institution's National Museum of Natural History. His footage from that trip was shared with the public in movie theaters.

Biologist **ROBERT E. COKER** (1876–1967) started his academic career with groundbreaking research that shed light on the optimal environment for oyster growth. He then was asked by the government of Peru to assess the potential for reviving its guano industry. His time among cormorants and other guano-producing birds provided many photographic opportunities. Coker spent the bulk of his career in the zoology department at the University of North Carolina at Chapel Hill.

For more than 35 years, photographer **DANIEL J. COX** has been hot on the trail of nature on all seven continents. His apparent kinship with owls resonates in the stunning images he provided for two cover stories, on the Great Gray Owl and the Snowy Owl, in *National Geographic*. Cox currently serves as volunteer director of the Arctic Documentary Project, for Polar Bears International.

Twins **FRANK CRAIGHEAD, JR.** ▼ (1916–2001), and **JOHN CRAIGHEAD** (1916–2016) first appeared in the pages of *National Geographic* as teenage falconers in the 1930s. They grew up to become two of the most famous wildlife biologists in the world, and for over half a century their wildlife photographs, ranging from those made in prewar India to those depicting the brothers' pioneering work with Yellowstone's grizzly bears and Golden Eagles, were published routinely in the magazine.

Ornithologist **ALLAN D. CRUICKSHANK** (1907–1974) spent many years as the official photographer of the National Audubon Society and contributed photos to more than 175 books. For his prolific coverage of birds, he was known as "Audubon with a camera," capturing images of some 550 different species of North American birds, a staggering figure even for today. He first became interested in birds at age 10, when he spotted a screech owl on Manhattan's West Side.

A member of a U.S. Navy Photo Unit and a graduate of the Navy diving school, **BILL CURTSINGER** was well prepared for his career as an underwater photographer. His unprecedented pictures of whales led in 1979 to his shooting on contract for National Geographic. His stunning depictions of marine mammals, gray reef sharks, sea turtles, shipwrecks, and the life of Arctic and Antarctic Seas have been gracing Society publications ever since.

At the age of 15, **BRUCE DALE** built a makeshift camera using old Agfa film and eyeglass lenses. In 1964 he joined the staff of National Geographic, where he had more than 2,000 images published during a 30-year career. Dale, who always had a talent for technical innovation, consulted with Nikon on early SLR cameras and was one of the first professionals to use digital photography. A Bruce Dale photograph was selected to journey on board NASA's Voyager spacecraft, to depict planet Earth.

By the age of 10, **FLIP DE NOOYER** (1948–2004) was a serious beginning birder and photographer in the Netherlands. He eventually would pursue his love of nature photography on all seven continents, specializing in mammals, birds, and landscapes, while also donating his time to conservation efforts in his home country. He was named BBC Wildlife Photographer of the Year in 1988 and 1989.

Growing up in the Galápagos Islands gave **TUI DE ROY** an unusual perspective. It allowed her to get to know very well the subjects of her many photographs of Galápagos wildlife, including the Blue-footed Booby. De Roy has traveled the world for decades in her photographic career, which blends strong advocacy with a deep, ethical concern for wildlife and their habitats. She is a founding fellow of the International League of Conservation Photographers.

DONALD R. DICKEY (1887–1932) was 16 years old when he hiked with a Sierra Club group that included naturalists John Muir and C. Hart Merriam. Dickey became a famed ornithologist, developed a remote camera for studying birds, and created films used by Howard Hughes's engineers to design airplanes. After her husband's death, Dickey's wife donated his entire bird and mammal collection—more than 70,000 specimens and 7,500 photographs—to the University of California, Los Angeles.

Famous as the man whose images froze bullets in mid-flight, **HAROLD E. "DOC" EDGERTON** (1903–1990), developer of the high-speed stroboscopic flash, was for many years a professor of electrical engineering at MIT. Yet he also worked closely with National Geographic, helping Jacques Cousteau improve deep-sea cameras, sonar transducers, and other imaging equipment. It was aboard the *Calypso* that Edgerton received the nickname Papa Flash.

DAVID EDWARDS has spent a lot of time in China and Mongolia in his 30-year career as a freelance photographer. He is known for his stunning photographs of Kazakh eagle hunters of western Mongolia, which appeared in a 1999 article in *National Geographic*. Behind the scenes, Edwards has organized a relief effort to provide winter clothing and medical supplies to impoverished Mongolians.

JASON EDWARDS began his career as a wildlife and natural history photographer working as a carnivore and primate husbandry specialist for the Zoological Board of Victoria, Australia. He is also highly regarded for remote landscape photography and his images of indigenous peoples. In 2004, Edwards was awarded the inaugural Pursuit of Excellence Award by the Australian Geographic Society for "his extreme efforts and absolute commitment to obtaining rare and amazing photographs."

Called "Toppy" because his father was head of the Topical Press Agency in London, **WALTER MEAYERS EDWARDS** (1908–1994) immigrated to the United States and joined the National Geographic staff in 1933. Over the next 40 years he served as picture editor, layout editor, chief of the illustrations division, promoter of underwater exploration, writer, and a photographer especially noted for his images of the desert Southwest.

Growing up in Colorado, **DAVID H. ELLIS** became fascinated by raptors early on in life. Later, he

chose the behavior of the Golden Eagle as the subject of his Ph.D. dissertation. His interest in birds of prey continues to take him all over the world and has led him to author more than a hundred publications. Ellis's research interests have also centered on cranes.

ROE ETHRIDGE studied photography at the Atlanta College of Art. His conceptual photographs often sample from or respond to the powerful visual culture of the 21st century to disrupt the typical narrative. His work has been exhibited at the Museum of Modern Art PS1 in New York and other contemporary art museums around the world.

Although known primarily for his sculpture, **PAUL J. FAIR** (1886–1953) was also active as a photographer in California, after moving there from Illinois as a young man. He immersed himself in the wildlife of his adopted state, providing *National Geographic* with a series of photos to illustrate a 1950 article on Sonoma's Valley of the Moon. Fair also worked in public relations for the U.S. Forest Service.

A transplanted Californian, **WILLIAM L. FINLEY** ▲ (1876–1953) dedicated his life to the appreciation and conservation of Oregon's birds. He began photographing them at an early age, joining up with his friend Herman T. Bohlman. The photographs and advocacy of Finley and Bohlman led to the creation of three Oregon wildlife refuges. After his death, Finley was honored with a namesake: the William L. Finley National Wildlife Refuge, in the Willamette Valley.

TIM FITZHARRIS is a former elementary and high school teacher who transitioned to a full-time photography career in 1979. He has alternated work in the field with teaching nature photography workshops and writing about the subject in his numerous books and as a monthly columnist for *Popular Photography & Imaging*. He has had a long working relationship with the Sierra Club and *Audubon* magazine, and his images have appeared in periodicals worldwide.

MARCELIN FLANDRIN (1889–1957) was born in Algeria and as a young man settled in Morocco. During World War I, he was involved in aerial observation and photography, and he carried that experience over into civilian life, as a pioneer in the aerial photography of Morocco. Flandrin lovingly documented the beauty of his adopted country, especially the iconic city of Casablanca.

JOHN E. "JACK" FLETCHER (1917–2003) joined the Geographic staff in 1944 and had a varied career, his assignments taking him as far as the Antarctic. He devised remotely triggered cameras to photograph rocket launches and became an expert in the electronic lighting of very large areas, his "monster flash" illuminating Piccadilly Circus, the Vienna State Opera, and the Houses of Parliament.

Both **MICHAEL AND PATRICIA FOGDEN** ► began their careers as research biologists with doctorates from Oxford and London Universities, respectively. Their collaboration started in 1968, and within 10 years they had transitioned to becoming freelance nature photojournalists with a specialty in rain forest subjects and a passion for hummingbirds.

Nebraska native **MICHAEL FORSBERG** shares his love of the Great Plains through his photography and his dedication to conservation efforts. In a career that has spanned more than 20 years, he has captured the beauty that remains in the formerly extensive and glorious grassland ecosystem, including the transitory presence of migrating Sandhill Cranes. In 2017, the Sierra Club awarded Forsberg the Ansel Adams Award for Conservation Photography.

Growing up along the shores of Lake Erie, **TODD FORSGREN** was inspired by the art of John James Audubon and Roger Tory Peterson, introduced to him by his birder parents. From 2006 to 2014, he worked with ornithological researchers to create portraits of 57 bird species caught in mist nets. He teaches his art at universities, workshops, and residencies, and has also trained his lenses on urban and community-based agriculture projects.

As a U.S. Army photographer in Vietnam, **GORDON GAHAN** (1945–1984) won two Bronze Stars and a Purple Heart while making the kind of images that in 1972 landed him a job on the National Geographic staff. For the next decade his varied assignments ranged from archaeology to natural history to photojournalism. In 1982, he went into advertising photography and, two years later, was killed in a helicopter crash while photographing in the Virgin Islands.

Growing up in Virginia, **RAYMOND GEHMAN** was always drawn to the outdoors. After graduating from the University of Missouri's School of Journalism and working for several newspapers, the former National Geographic photo intern began shooting for the Society's publications on a freelance basis. He has photographed features on wildlife, wetlands, fire ecology, prairie dogs, and the destruction caused by Hurricane Andrew in 1992.

ROBBIE GEORGE honed his love of nature during a childhood spent in Aspen, Colorado. As a photographer, he blends the conservation of nature and wildlife with his professional endeavors to ensure that future generations can enjoy nature's splendors. Now based in Maine, the widely published George is noted for his intimate wildlife photos and exquisite landscapes.

A native of Cincinnati, **ROBERT B. GOODMAN** (1933–1998) was an adventuresome photographer. An early assignment for *National Geographic* had him shooting close to the mouth of a volcano. Goodman has also worked well with explorers, accompanying world-ranging mariner Alan Villiers and the most famous of undersea adventurers, Jacques Cousteau. For a 1964 cover story, Goodman documented the experiences of the oceanauts in Continental Shelf Station Two, a submerged colony in the Red Sea.

Having roamed the world as a photographer, **SERGEY GORSHKOV** is always drawn back to the natural beauty of his native Russia, especially that of the Kamchatka Peninsula. He finds particular inspiration in Kamchatka's bears, and has captured the huge mammals engaging in the activities of their yearly cycle, from fishing in the salmon run to raising cubs. Of his craft, Gorshkov says, "Nature is my main teacher and I'm still taking lessons."

Botswana-based **VINCENT GRAFHORST** was born in the Netherlands. Choosing civil engineering and construction as a field, he moved in 1998 to South Africa in search of adventure, and not long after made Botswana his home. Inspired by the images of Frans Lanting and others, Grafhorst made a serious transition to photography, specializing in wildlife and landscapes.

GEORGE GRALL has been fascinated by snakes, toads, and other crawling creatures since he was three years old, so waiting a week in a New Guinea rain forest for one picture of a frog came to him naturally. Such patience has allowed Grall to photograph seahorses, snapping turtles, the invertebrates clustering on a Chesapeake wharf piling, and the creatures of the Chihuahuan Desert for a variety of National Geographic publications.

CLEVELAND P. GRANT (1904–1985) was born in Wisconsin and was a curator at the Field Museum of Natural History in Chicago. However, he is best known for his documentaries of wild birds and animals, which he filmed and edited in collaboration with his wife and business partner, Ruth Halverson Grant. Grant was one of the primary contributors to the Disney "shot-in-the-wild" adventure movies of the 1950s and went on six safaris to film wildlife in Africa.

Although his work takes him far and wide, English photographer **DANNY GREEN** enjoys shooting in the United Kingdom, where even familiar locations can be full of surprises. He is most content among the seabird colonies of the Shetland Islands. Green's intimate images of puffin domestic life, acquired over a period of five years, formed the basis for the June 2014 *National Geographic* article "Puffin Therapy."

CRAWFORD H. GREENEWALT (1902–1993) was a chemical engineer by training and eventually the president and chairman of the board of DuPont. Still, he found time in his busy life to pursue two of his passions: ornithology and high-speed photography. He needed more than a working knowledge of the latter, and fortunately had the assistance of his friend Harold E. "Doc" Edgerton, to photograph the hummingbirds he pursued throughout the Americas.

Still in his mid-20s, **BERTIE GREGORY** ◄ has a résumé even seasoned professional photographers would envy. He is both an accomplished photographer and a cinematographer and has been named a Scientific Exploration Society Zenith Explorer and a National Geographic Young Explorer. He has assisted National Geographic photographer Steve Winter in South Africa, India, and Sri Lanka. He is currently affiliated with the BBC's Natural History Unit and is the host of the National Geographic WILD digital show *wild_life.*

Originally a painter and sculptor, **FARRELL GREHAN** found a new line of work when he began photographing the teeming life of New York City. This led to a stint as a *Life* magazine stringer, followed by a dozen years shooting freelance for National Geographic. His stories have ranged from biographical tributes to Thoreau, Willa Cather, and Teddy Roosevelt to articles on the Mazatzal wilderness in Arizona.

A Minnesota native, **ANNIE GRIFFITHS** ▲ majored in journalism before working as a photographer for the *Minnesota Daily* and the *Worthington Daily Globe.* By 1978, she was shooting on contract for National Geographic, and over the next several decades her assignments have ranged from the Middle East (Lawrence of Arabia, Jerusalem, Petra, Galilee) to England's Lake District to the back roads of America.

Like his father, Melville Bell Grosvenor, and grandfather Gilbert H. Grosvenor, **GILBERT MELVILLE GROSVENOR** has served both as editor of *National Geographic* (1970–1980) and president of the Society (1980–1996). After joining the staff in 1954, he spent a number of years, when not picture editing, on photographic assignments. He was often accompanied by his wife, the accomplished photographer **DONNA K. GROSVENOR**, whose own photos have illustrated articles and books.

ROBERT B. "BOBBY" HAAS has achieved something many people only dream of: a second career as a National Geographic photographer. A successful financier, Haas has embarked on experiments in aerial photography on continental scales. His dramatic, stirring images of African animals and his South American landscapes seen from the vantage of the sky have been published by the Society as books, including *Through the Eyes of the Gods* and *Through the Eyes of the Condor*.

Wildlife photographer **JONATHAN HARROD** is also a marine scientist, avid conservationist, and bird enthusiast. He grew up in Sydney, Australia, and moved to New Zealand in 2008, where he now lives, in Christchurch, on the South Island. He is especially interested in observing and documenting the behavior of rare and endangered bird species living in that part of the world. His photograph of Bar-tailed Godwits accompanied a *National Geographic* story on bird migration in 2018.

While still relatively new to the trade, **DAVID ALAN HARVEY** received an arts fellowship that steered him from black-and-white newspaper photography to color magazine photography. At heart he remained a photojournalist, and over the past four decades he has completed more than 60 assignments for *National Geographic*, including extensive work in Cuba. Born in 1944, he bought his first camera with savings from his paper route. Intent on mentoring emerging photographers, he teaches workshops and, in 2008, founded *burn*, an online photography magazine.

A Japanese wildlife photographer, **TSUNEO HAYASHIDA** specializes in capturing images of cranes the world over, celebrating them for their beauty and symbolism in his home culture. Once called the doyen of Japanese crane photography, he contributed the photographs and text for a story in *National Geographic* magazine in 1983, "The Japanese Crane, Bird of Happiness," and also created two books on cranes. His photograph of a pair of mating cranes once appeared on Japan's 1,000-yen note.

FRANCIS H. HERRICK (1858–1940) was a naturalist who founded the department of biology at Case Western Reserve University. Professor Herrick's first contribution to *National Geographic* was a report on the condition of wood from a buried forest at Muir Inlet, Alaska, in 1892. He later wrote and photographed the magazine's May 1929 story "The Eagle in Action: An Intimate Study of the Eyrie Life of America's National Bird," based on years of observations from an 80-foot steel tower erected near a lively Bald Eagle eyrie outside Cleveland, Ohio.

SAM HOBSON is a British wildlife and conservation photographer best known for his close-up portraits of urban wildlife, often captured using remote triggers or camera traps. Hobson won the prestigious Wildlife Photographer of the Year award in 2014 and 2016. He specializes in images that tell a story, crafting photographs that convey the relationship between the subject and its environment.

RALPH LEE HOPKINS is the founder and director of the expedition photography program for National Geographic's Lindblad Expeditions. For more than 25 years he has photographed expeditions to the Arctic, the Antarctic, and points in between. His background in geology makes him especially sensitive to wild landscapes. He has written and illustrated guidebooks to geology in the American West and a handbook on taking great nature photographs.

JAMES FRANCIS "FRANK" HURLEY (1885–1962) was an Australian photographer and filmmaker known for his daring work on expeditions and in wartime. In 1914–17 he took a second trip to Antarctica, this time with Sir Ernest Shackleton, making historic photographs of the *Endurance* expedition. As official photographer for the Australian Imperial Force, he documented battles from the ground and the air. Although his somewhat sensational films of native life in Papua New Guinea were controversial, his services in connection with the war won him the Order of the British Empire in 1941.

OTIS IMBODEN (1928–2006) had hardly joined the *National Geographic* staff in 1961 when he was detailed to cover the space program at Cape Canaveral, an assignment that lasted the better part of a decade. A Memphis boy who had a master's degree in English literature, Imboden won the Apollo Achievement Award for his efforts and went on to photograph drowned galleons, the Everglades, ancient Maya ruins, and experimental sailplanes before retiring in 1986.

Nature photographer **MITSUAKI IWAGO** ▼ charmed the Internet world with his *World Cats Travelogue,* a 2012 video presentation, and he continues to photograph cats around the world. Working with Olympus, he has also spearheaded a Global Warming Witness photography project, chronicling evidence of climate change worldwide and inspiring other photographers to do the same. His photographs from Africa's Serengeti Plain appeared in the May 1986 issue of *National Geographic.* He lives in Tokyo, Japan.

CHARLIE HAMILTON JAMES is a Britain-based photographer and filmmaker who specializes in subjects related to conservation and anthropology. He has spent more than two decades exploring Peru's Amazonian rain forest, and he was one of the six photographers who covered Yellowstone for *National Geographic*'s May 2016 issue. His raw photographs of vultures illustrated a January 2016 story. He draws crowds with his *National Geographic Live* lectures, including the recent one, "I Bought a Rain Forest."

Since first shooting as a freelancer in 1983, **CHRIS JOHNS** has pursued photographic assignments around the globe, from the American West to Africa's Kalahari Desert and Great Rift Valley. He joined the National Geographic staff in 1995 and served as editor in chief of the magazine from 2005 to 2014. His photographs can be found in the collections of Bill Gates and the late Nelson Mandela. In 2003, *American Photo* magazine named him one of world's 25 most important photographers.

After 30 years as a photojournalist, **LYNN JOHNSON** feels that she is now moving from "observer to advocate" because, as she puts it, "the people are more important than the photographs." Johnson commits herself so completely to the communities she encounters that this attitude has lent her pictures an especially sensitive touch—including photographs accompanying such hard-hitting *National Geographic* stories as those about the threat of worldwide pandemics and weapons of mass destruction.

For nearly two decades, starting in 1972, **DEWITT JONES** was a steady freelance contributor to *National Geographic*, known for evocative pieces on the wilderness vision of John Muir, the New England celebrated by Robert Frost, the majestic California redwoods, and the mysterious Anasazi people who once thrived in the desert Southwest.

He now works as an inspirational speaker and trainer with the message "Celebrate what's right."

A native of Sweden, **MATTIAS KLUM** is internationally renowned as an activist who uses nature photography and videography to raise awareness and effect change. His stories for *National Geographic* include a feature on meerkats and a report on the ecological crisis in Borneo. He has created eight films and 14 books, including, with Johan Rockström, *Big World, Small Planet*, praised in a *New York Times* op-ed by Thomas L. Friedman for "stunning photographs of ecosystem disruptions [that] reinforce the urgency of the moment."

FRANKLIN PRICE KNOTT (1854–1930) was a pioneer in the early 20th-century process called Autochrome and contributed some of the first color photographs to *National Geographic*, starting in 1916 with a suite of 32 images accompanying Gilbert H. Grosvenor's article on the United States, "The Land of the Best," and continuing later that year with color images of people and places around the world, from a Tunisian blacksmith to the Taj Mahal.

KENT KOBERSTEEN was the director of photography for *National Geographic* from 1987 to 2005. He had already established himself as a photojournalist, working 18 years as a photographer and editor for the *Minneapolis Tribune*. When asked in 2012 what it took to be a National Geographic photographer, he answered with four words: intellect, passion, maturity, and drive. Kobersteen now leads photography workshops and lectures extensively on the philosophy, ethics, and business of photojournalism.

Best known for his studies of endangered species, **CARL B. KOFORD** (1915–1979) spent time in Panama and Puerto Rico but worked primarily with natural history museums in his capacity as a biologist and researcher at the University of California, Berkeley. From the late 1930s on, he spent years observing the decline of the California Condor, work that resulted in a historic monograph published by the National Audubon Society in 1953. At that time, Koford estimated there were only 60 condors remaining.

An award-winning freelance photographer, **BOB KRIST** has been stranded on a glacier in Iceland, nearly run down by charging bulls in southern India, and knighted with a cutlass during a Trinidadian voodoo ceremony. He is a contributing editor of *National Geographic Traveler*, and the Society of American Travel Writers has three times named him Travel Photographer of the Year. A book containing his photographs, Frances Mayes's *Tuscany*, spent a month on the *New York Times* Best Sellers list.

KEITH LADZINSKI is an acclaimed photographer and filmmaker whose quest for extreme adventure and out-of-the-way landscapes has taken him to all seven continents. One of his specialties is photographing the world's top rock climbers, assignments for which he hazards death-defying heights. In 2012 he accompanied writer Freddie Wilkinson and fellow photographer Cory Richards on a hair-raising expedition to Antarctica's Queen Maud Land.

TIM LAMAN ▲ is a wildlife photographer, filmmaker, and field biologist with a Harvard Ph.D. in ornithology. By doggedly tracking birds-of-paradise in Papua New Guinea and orangutans in Borneo, sitting high in the rain forest canopy and setting up complex computer-driven cameras, Laman has captured images of behaviors never before photographed. He and fellow ornithologist Edwin Scholes catalogued all 39 bird-of-paradise species for a National Geographic book published in 2012.

Born in Holland, **FRANS LANTING** is a celebrated nature and wildlife photographer whose work appears frequently in National Geographic books and magazines. He has photographed bonobos in tropical Africa, lemurs in Madagascar, volcanoes in Hawaii, and penguins in Antarctica. He spent a year photographing around the world for a 1999 special *National Geographic* millennium issue focusing on biodiversity. A renowned speaker and creative collaborator, he has partnered with an aboriginal painter and the composer Philip Glass.

A National Geographic staff photographer from 1974 to 1987, **BIANCA LAVIES** ▶ specialized in natural history subjects, the more bizarre the better. She slithered among snakes, ventured among "killer" bees, explored the world of a compost pile, and photographed millions of monarch butterflies clustered in their Mexican winter haven. Born in Holland, Lavies wandered New Zealand and South Africa before arriving in the United States after crossing the Atlantic in a 30-foot sailing boat.

DAVID LIITTSCHWAGER is a wildlife photographer with a unique provenance: He came from the world of advertising, having worked with Richard Avedon in New York City. He now applies techniques of portraiture to natural history subjects as small as zooplankton, with the aim of depicting even the tiniest animal as an individual. His studies of marine microfauna, octopuses, and other creatures often appear in National Geographic books and articles.

BATES LITTLEHALES was an early master of 35-mm underwater photography. The Princeton graduate was given his first diving lesson shortly after joining the Society's staff in 1952. He photographed the activities of Jacques Cousteau and other deep-sea pioneers and marine archaeologists and designed the OceanEye, a highly praised underwater camera housing. Littlehales retired in 1989 after 37 years as a National Geographic staff photographer, yet he is still highly regarded as a bird photographer.

MICHAEL E. LONG (1932–2015) was a photographer, writer, and editor on the National Geographic staff from 1966 to 1994 and continued to write for the magazine well past 2000. His photograph of the Sydney Opera House is among those Carl Sagan had inscribed in the Golden Records carried by the Voyager spacecraft out into the universe. Long was an accomplished aviator, and his credits reflect his interest in flight and space exploration as well as nature.

A graduate of the University of Missouri School of Journalism, **ROBERT MADDEN** was a National Geographic photographic intern in 1967 and returned as a staff member in 1973, publishing more than 20 stories from locations as disparate as the Venezuela rain forest and Brooklyn, New York. For the next decade his assignments carried him across the United States, down to Antarctica, and into a newly opened China. His coverage of the 1976 Guatemalan earthquake was honored with an Overseas Press Club award.

Considered by most the quintessential National Geographic correspondent, **LUIS MARDEN** (1913–2003) dove with Jacques Cousteau, found the wreck of the H.M.S. *Bounty* in the South Pacific, witnessed NASA rocket launches, and made numerous natural history discoveries: an orchid in Brazil, prehistoric fossil eggs in Madagascar, a lobster parasite in New England waters. He not only pioneered underwater photography but also introduced 35-mm cameras and Kodachrome film at National Geographic.

GREG MARSHALL is a marine biologist, photographer, and filmmaker who invented Crittercam, a system of animal-borne cameras that captures video of the world through animals' eyes. His work has been featured in numerous films covering

more than 70 species, from Emperor Penguins to blue whales and from house cats to grizzly bears. Marshall has collaborated with dozens of scientists worldwide to study behavioral and ecological questions using remote-imaging technology.

ARTHUR ELLIS MAYER (dates unknown) wrote articles on the technology of photographic techniques and equipment in the early 20th century. He contributed an essay on the value of and methods for enlarging photographs to the 1909 *American Annual of Photography*. His August 1913 *National Geographic* article, "Gems of the Italian Lakes," included photographs of magnificent peacocks at the historic Isola Bella, one of the Borromean Islands, near the Italy-Switzerland border.

The name of National Geographic staff photographer **DONALD MCBAIN** (dates unknown) has recently resurfaced as people have discovered his 1957 photograph of a zookeeper feeding a hippo, the animal's massive jaws spread wide open. With Robert F. Sisson, McBain created the photographs for a 28-page feature on the National Zoo in the magazine's April 1957 issue.

Wildlife photographer **GRAHAM MCGEORGE** was born in Dumfries, Scotland, and now lives in Jacksonville, Florida. His photograph of a grinning seal won him a commendation in the Comedy Wildlife Photography Awards, and his series of photographs of screech owls nestled in knotholes, titled "Masters of Disguise," has been shared far and wide for its fascinating glimpse of bird behavior and camouflage.

A native of the Netherlands, **WIL MEINDERTS** considers himself an "all-round nature photographer," known for stunning landscapes of wild places, close-up portraits of animals (both on land and underwater), and pleasing arrangements of natural objects such as seashells. He has created wildlife photographs from around the world, both in his European homeland and in tropical locations such as the Seychelles.

Torn between engineering and art while at Syracuse University, **MICHAEL MELFORD** picked up a camera and his problem was resolved. As a freelance photographer who has shot prolifically for National Geographic since 1990, Melford can unite his mechanical side with his creative bent. He has focused his art and craft on places of scenic grandeur such as national parks and historical sites, and increasingly on threatened wilderness areas.

After 27 years in the software industry, **MICHAEL MILICIA** began his second career as a nature photographer specializing in wildlife, especially birds. His work has won him recognition from the North American Nature Photography Association and in *Audubon* magazine competitions. His background in computer science gives him a technical bent, which he puts to use in his popular photography classes and workshops.

STEVE MILLS is an award-winning photographer based in North Yorkshire, England, who specializes in birds. His work is precise yet emotional, showing off both the beauty and the personality of the birds on the other end of his lens. He has written a field guide to bird-watching in northern Greece, and co-founded BirdWING, an organization created to protect wildlife habitats in Greece.

Discharged from the U.S. Air Force, **GEORGE F. MOBLEY** decided to become a photojournalist, so he earned a degree from the University of Missouri and, in 1961, landed a job as a staff photographer with National Geographic. For the next 33 years, his assignments took him around the world, but no place in Asia, Africa, or Europe enchanted him quite as much as those regions with which his work is most closely intertwined, the Arctic and Antarctica.

Originally **MARK MOFFETT** taught himself macrophotography to better document his Harvard Ph.D. dissertation on Asian marauder ants. The superb artistry of his pictures, however, soon won them a spot in *National Geographic*. Ever since, Moffett has been training his lenses not just on all manner of ants but also on jumping spiders, poison dart frogs, mantids, and entire ecosystems that might clothe just one giant forest tree.

Born in Hungary but raised in Pittsburgh, **ALBERT MOLDVAY** (1921–1995) was a photographer for the *Denver Post* before joining the Society's staff in 1961. He then spent five months in Antarctica, prelude to a decade of assignments that included Spain, the Italian Riviera, New York City, and (with the U.S. Air Force) Vietnam. After resigning in 1972, he established an independent business and wrote a syndicated photography column.

She came from Poland by way of New York City; he hailed from New Zealand but arrived from London. Yet once **YVA MOMATIUK** and **JOHN EASTCOTT** ▼ met in Wyoming, they were finally able to forge the partnership that has made them the esteemed writers and photographers they are today. Known for their work on indigenous peoples and natural history subjects, in 1976 the pair began working freelance for *National Geographic*, covering stories whose subjects ranged from the Inuit communities of the Arctic to the high mountains of their respective homelands.

A Michigan farm boy, **W. ROBERT MOORE** (1899–1968) worked for Detroit newspapers and taught science in Thailand (then known as Siam) before his photography landed him a job with *National Geographic* in 1931. He became chief of its foreign editorial staff and had a hand in nearly 90 articles on places from around the world before retiring in 1967. In 1937, he shot the magazine's first Kodachrome photographs (action color photography on 35-mm film).

VINCENT MUNIER came to love old trees, windswept mountains, and snowy wilderness while growing up in France's Vosges region. He specializes in photographs that surprise and mystify, and he travels the world to find them. He was named BBC Wildlife Photographer of the Year three years in a row, 2000–2002. His 2015 book, *Arctique*, and a short film showcased on the National Geographic website both feature his efforts to capture the scenery and animal life of the Arctic.

Born in Brooklyn and a longtime resident of Long Island, **ROBERT CUSHMAN MURPHY** (1887–1973) was a trailblazing environmental activist and curator of oceanic birds at New York's American Museum of Natural History. He inspired Rachel Carson's *Silent Spring*, the book that in turn inspired the modern-day environmental movement. Two mountains, a park, a spider, a planet, three species of birds, and more have been named after him. Over several decades, Murphy contributed stories and photographs to *National Geographic* from Peru, Polynesia, Ireland, and elsewhere.

Born in Sewickley, Pennsylvania, **VINCENT J. MUSI** secured his first real newspaper job just upriver, at the *Pittsburgh Press*, remaining there for nearly a decade. In 1993 he began freelancing for *National Geographic*, where his assignments have spanned a great range of subjects. Musi has photographed Route 66, West Indian volcanoes, the Texas Hill Country, Wales, animal cognition, and the mummy-strewn catacombs of Palermo, Sicily.

Over the years, **MICHAEL "NICK" NICHOLS** has contributed some 30 stories to *National Geographic*. He has worked as a staff photographer since 1996 and editor at large for photography since 2008. From 1999 to 2002, Nichols accompanied explorer Mike Fay on his megatransect of Africa's largest stretch of continuous rain forest. His depiction of Gabon's rain forest inspired the creation of 13 national parks, and his portrayal of elephants in Chad raised public awareness and funding to protect them. In 2012 the magazine published his groundbreaking 84-image composite photograph of a 300-foot-tall giant sequoia.

A Canadian-born marine biologist, **PAUL NICKLEN ▸** spent his childhood among the Inuit people, who taught him to survive in icy ecosystems. Much of his work focuses on polar wildlife and climate change, and his depictions of wildlife on and under the frozen surface of the world's polar oceans have become regular features in National Geographic publications. He won international acclaim in 2006 for his story of a leopard seal in Antarctica who insisted on feeding him while he took photos of her.

At the age of 28, **ERNST NIEBERGALL** (1876–1954) traveled alone from his birthplace in Germany and soon settled in Sandusky, Ohio, where he lived the rest of his life. His photography reflects the everyday life and natural surroundings of the Lake Erie shoreline of the 20th century. His camera equipment, film and glass negatives, and photographic ledgers are now preserved at the Rutherford B. Hayes Presidential Center in Fremont, Ohio.

KLAUS NIGGE was for many years a wildlife biologist before turning to nature photography full time. A painstaking craftsman, the German-born Nigge is a self-described "slow photographer," patient in his approach and ingenious in the construction of his blinds. He has photographed animals ranging from bears to the rare European bison, and his pictures of pelicans, Steller's Sea Eagles, and the endangered Philippine Eagle have been published in *National Geographic*.

A versatile photojournalist, **RANDY OLSON** has worked for National Geographic since 1990, completing more than 30 assignments. One of only two people named Photographer of the Year in both the newspaper and magazine category of the Pictures of the Year International competition, Olson has produced stories on remote Siberia, consumerism in China, ancient Black Sea shipwrecks, the depletion of global fisheries, and the conflict between park and people on the Serengeti. His wife, Melissa Farlow, is also a National Geographic photographer.

PETE OXFORD travels the world making photographs in the most pristine wildlife spots and remotest cultural destinations. Though born in Britain, he has lived in Ecuador for more than 30 years. His education as a biologist infuses his photography, which he sees as a vital tool for conservation. Oxford works in tandem with his wife, photographer Renee Bish, and together they organize expeditions, offering "responsible travel to some of the world's richest cultures and most biodiverse and pristine areas of our planet."

WINFIELD PARKS (1932–1977), a native of Rhode Island and a former navy cameraman in Korea, was a photographer for the *Providence Journal-Bulletin* before he joined the staff of National Geographic in 1961. For the next 15 years, Parks's assignments took him to some 40 countries, where he wasn't afraid to risk his life for his work, once dangling from a helicopter 2,000 feet above Singapore just to get the best pictures. His photographs won acclaim for him and the magazine. Tragically, he died of a sudden heart attack at the age of 45.

Originally trained as a marine biologist, **THOMAS P. PESCHAK** left science in 2004 to become a photographer, using his award-winning work to strengthen conservation efforts, especially in the oceans. He has written and shot photos for five books. One of his most renowned photographs shows a researcher sitting shirtless in a kayak, followed closely by a great white shark three times the kayak's size. His six *National Geographic* stories have taken readers underwater in China, Mozambique, South Africa, Oman, and the Seychelles.

WILLIAM J. PETERS (1863–1942) was a scientist and explorer whose early work was for the U.S. Geological Survey in Alaska, where several place-names still reflect his significance there. He represented the National Geographic Society on the Ziegler Polar Expedition, 1903–1905, which aimed to reach the North Pole but did not succeed because of extreme weather conditions. Later, working for the Carnegie Institution, he sailed more than 100,000 nautical miles, using precise magnetic equipment to correct navigational charts.

A Hungarian photographer educated as a biologist, **JOE PETERSBURGER** specializes in images of rare plants and animals in eastern Europe, although he has traveled the world in search of wildlife to study and photograph. His portfolio includes remarkable close-up and stop-motion images of birds and insects. His coverage of the endangered long-tailed mayfly made him the first Hungarian citizen to publish a story in *National Geographic*, and he has contributed stories and photographs ever since.

AL PETTEWAY and **AMY WHITE** are best known as musicians. Performing on guitar and other string instruments, they have won a Grammy and an Indie for their Celtic-Appalachian blended sound. Yet they also make photographs, sharing the wildlife and vistas from their North Carolina mountaintop home. Deciding to combine their artistic talents, the two now offer musical performances against a backdrop of their nature photography.

A New York lawyer, **CHARLES HARRIS PHELPS** (1845–date unknown) traveled the Volga River in 1873, returning with a report for the American Geographical Society, including photographs now part of the National Geographic Image Collection. He and his wife made another adventurous journey in the 1880s, from Japan, China, and India through the Khyber Pass to remote sites in the Middle East, where, as Phelps wrote the Harvard alumni secretary, "my wife was the first European lady ever seen in the city and hundreds followed us through the streets."

Captain **HARRY PIDGEON** (1869–1954) says that he left his work as a "photographer among the great trees of the Sierras," spent 18 months and a thousand dollars to ready his yawl, and set sail from San Clemente, taking photographs whenever a picture-worthy scene presented itself. The February 1928 issue of *National Geographic* included a 33-page feature on this journey, titled "Around the World in the 'Islander': A Narrative of the Adventures of a Solitary Voyager on his Four-Year Cruise in a Thirty-Four-Foot Sailing Craft."

DIETER PLAGE (1936–1993) and his wife, **MARY GRANT PLAGE**, worked together as a team, writing and photographing on assignment for National Geographic from locations including Java, Sri Lanka, and the Galápagos. They also produced numerous wildlife documentaries for the United Kingdom version of the television series *Survival*. Dieter Plage died tragically during an aerial filming exercise in Sumatra, an event depicted in Werner Herzog's film *The White Diamond*.

HERBERT G. PONTING ▾ (1870–1935) was the first professional photographer in the Antarctic, and the first person to make a film there. Ponting documented Robert F. Scott's Terra Nova Expedition from 1910 to 1913. He spent 14 months in Antarctica and returned to Britain with 1,700 glass-plate negatives—but Scott did not, leaving Ponting with a poignant photographic narrative of the tragic expedition. Ponting published a book, *The Great White South*; created two films, one silent; and contributed two sets of photos to National Geographic, all about the expedition.

Educated as an engineer but an artist at heart, **MANUEL PRESTI** has been winning awards as one of the world's top wildlife photographers for more than a decade. Born in Italy, he enjoys seeking wildlife in the city of Rome, which is where he took his famous photograph titled "Sky Chase," showing a flock of starlings interrupted by a Peregrine Falcon. In 2005 the shot won him the prestigious title BBC Wildlife Photographer of the Year.

A noted wildlife photographer, **MICHAEL S. QUINTON** grew up in Idaho and taught himself the rudiments of cameras and lenses so that he might better indulge his interest in the natural world. He has lived near Yellowstone and in Alaska, and his photographs of many bird species (Great Gray Owls, goshawks, loons, ravens, and flickers, among others) have been published in *National Geographic*.

NIALL RANKIN (1904–1965) was deemed "one of Great Britain's leading wildlife photographers" when he contributed his photographic story "A Naturalist in Penguin Land" to the January 1955 *National Geographic*. For the expedition behind the story, he transported his 42-foot cruiser *Albatross* by whaling vessel to the Falkland Island of South Georgia and then spent five months circumnavigating the island, coming upon tens of thousands of penguins at a time. At the time of his death, a British birding journal lamented that "he published little and exhibited even less."

STEVE RAYMER earned a master's degree in journalism, studied Soviet and Russian affairs at Stanford University, and served as a lieutenant in the Vietnam War. He joined the National Geographic staff in 1972 to cover the story behind the story, going to the site of breaking news around the world, including the global hunger crisis, the Alaska pipeline, the Chernobyl nuclear accident, and the work of the Red Cross. His courage and artistry have won him acclaim and awards. He is now professor emeritus at Indiana University's Media School.

Dutch-born **ROBERT REIJNEN** has been a passionate nature photographer for 40 years. He calls his work "an uncontrolled hobby," yet it has gained recognition and reached prizewinning status. The Museum Ton Schulten, in Ootmarsum, Netherlands, staged a recent exhibition of his work.

Called mild-mannered and self-effacing by those who knew him, **J. BAYLOR ROBERTS** (1902–1994) was one of the most stalwart *National Geographic* photographers of the 20th century, on the staff and ready to travel from 1936 to 1967. He contributed to nearly 60 stories during those years, starting in the 1930s at home, with pieces on American agriculture, but soon traveling to the Philippines, Singapore, Iran, and Hong Kong, and beyond, sending back photographs for the magazine.

JOSEPH F. ROCK (1884–1962) was an eccentric botanist. Born in Vienna, he spent 27 years in the remote Tibetan borderlands, collecting exotic plants while dodging warlords, eluding bandits, parlaying with lamas, and photographing little-known peoples and ceremonies. He contributed 10 articles to *National Geographic*, with titles that included phrases such as "An American Agricultural Explorer Makes His Way Through Brigand-infested Central China." Three different plant species and the herbarium at the University of Hawaii at Manoa are named after him.

As a young photographer, **NORBERT ROSING** fell in love first with Scandinavia and then with the Arctic. He has photographed all the creatures of the far north: walruses, musk oxen, whales, Arctic foxes, and polar bear. His first cover story in *National Geographic*, "Bear Beginnings: New Life on the Ice," was published in December 2000. He is also devoted to photographing the national parks of his native Germany.

EDWARD S. ROSS (1915–2016) was a world-renowned entomologist, a specialist in embiids (web-spinning insects), or what Ross called "small game," and for 75 years curator, chairman, and then emeritus at the California Academy of Sciences. Early on he planned to become an illustrator, and that artistic bent drove his lifelong talent for close-up photography. Over the years, he contributed stories or photographs to *National Geographic* on insects, flowers, and their interactions—and once, on birds.

ALEX SABERI hails from London, where he honed his fine art technique photographing stately Richmond Park. Recognized as among the best photographers in the United Kingdom, Saberi has traveled to Brazil, Cuba, Bolivia, Iceland, Sri Lanka, and beyond, capturing dramatic scenes of wildlife, landscapes, people, and nature against atmospheric backdrops.

At 16, **BARNET SAIDMAN** (1913–1993) lied about his age to get a job with the *Bristol Evening World*, thus beginning a lifelong career as a cameraman at several London newspapers and chief photographer at the *News Chronicle*. A notorious perfectionist and versatile photographer, Saidman shot sporting events, portraits of the royal family, architecture, and the battlefields of World War II, where he served as a Royal Air Force officer.

KIYOSHI SAKAMOTO began contributing photographs from a now bygone Japan to *National Geographic* in the early 1920s. A schoolteacher with a flair for photography, he was soon sending prints constantly from his Tokyo home. Editors brought him to Washington, D.C., to learn the Autochrome process, to add color to his work. He mastered the art, providing delicately colored photographs to the magazine, and in 1929 was recognized at the Photographic Fine Arts Exhibition in Osaka.

JOEL SARTORE, ▼ a former newspaperman who grew up in Nebraska, began freelancing for National Geographic in 1992, his numerous assignments centering on complex ecological stories. Endangered species, endangered parkland, the lost Ivory-billed Woodpecker, the countdown to extinction—Sartore cannot help but see in his pictures a rapidly vanishing world: "It's really the last of everything I'm photographing." Sartore's much-loved animal portraits come from the Photo Ark, his multiyear mission to document a world worth saving.

Originally trained as a seabird biologist, **KEVIN SCHAFER** has been a professional natural history photographer and writer for 30 years. He has specialized in documenting threatened ecosystems and endangered species on all seven continents, especially in the tropical rain forest and polar regions. Schafer is a founding fellow of the International League of Conservation Photographers.

The five years (1964–69) that **FRANK** (1924–1994) and **HELEN SCHREIDER** were on the National Geographic staff were but one chapter in a shared life of travel. As a young couple, they drove amphibious jeeps on long rambles in exotic locales, writing and taking pictures. For them, the thrill was irresistible. The Geographic published articles on their wanderings across Indonesia, the Great Rift Valley, and the Near East. The couple continued their vagabond ways until Frank's death during a voyage on the Aegean Sea.

PHIL SCHERMEISTER first picked up a camera in college and worked as a newspaper photographer for many years before going freelance. He has photographed on assignment in more than 40 national parks around the United States and has published six single-artist photography books with National Geographic. Some of his other assignments have included coverage of American Indians in the Andes of Peru and Mexico's Copper Canyon.

JOHN SCOFIELD (1914–1996) was a U.S. Army captain in World War II and a self-taught journalist with no formal education, but a passion for travel. He joined the National Geographic staff in 1953 and stayed for 25 years, often serving as both writer and photographer on his articles, which number more than 20. Scofield was on the senior editorial staff under Gilbert M. Grosvenor and led expeditions into Israel, Bhutan, Haiti, New Guinea, and Hong Kong.

Turkish ornithologist and conservation ecologist **CAGAN H. SEKERCIOGLU** has seen 55 percent of the planet's birds. Working in biodiversity hot spots such as Costa Rica, Turkey, Ethiopia, Nepal, and Tanzania, Sekercioglu tracks the causes and consequences of vanishing bird populations, habitat loss, and climate change. By compiling a global bird database from his own fieldwork and scientific literature, he has been able to estimate extinction trends on a global scale. He also directs a grassroots conservation organization in Turkey called KuzeyDoga and was named a National Geographic Emerging Explorer in 2011.

Award-winning wildlife photographer and author **ANUP SHAH**, who grew up in Kenya, has shot eight feature stories for *National Geographic*. By fully immersing himself in national parks for years on end, Shah has been able to capture unexpected

movements in photos that ring with intensity. His artful images provide an intimate view of Bengal tigers in Ranthambore National Park, elephants and lions in Serengeti-Maasai Mara, and the chimpanzees of Gombe National Park.

As a young man in the 1880s, **GEORGE SHIRAS 3D** ▸ (1859–1942) put away his gun and began "hunting with a camera." Wildlife photography was virtually nonexistent, but he pioneered methods and techniques, especially flashlight photography at night, to produce images that remain breathtaking today. Beginning in 1906 and for several decades thereafter, his pictures were seen by millions in the pages of *National Geographic*.

An expert naturalist with everlasting patience, writer-photographer **ROBERT F. SISSON** (1923–2002) favored the little things in life. He would haul bulky camera gear into the wild in search of a singular flower or insect. A fiend for accuracy, he typically spent a year and a half writing one story. In 1961, President John F. Kennedy presented him with a medal for winning that year's White House News Photographers Association competition.

Over the past 30 years, marine wildlife specialist **BRIAN SKERRY** has spent more than 10,000 hours underwater. A photographer for *National Geographic* since 1998, he was named a National Geographic Fellow in 2014. Skerry's creative images tell stories that not only celebrate the mystery and beauty of the sea but also help bring attention to the many issues that endanger our oceans.

WILBUR F. SMITH (1851–1937) served as the fish and game warden for Fairfield County in Connecticut and was a leader in both bird photography and conservation. Seeing that birds offered unique services to a healthy ecosystem, Smith educated the public on how best to attract beneficial birds to their homes, gardens, and farms. His photography appeared in *Bird Lore*, a magazine of the Audubon Society devoted to the study and protection of birds.

JAMES L. STANFIELD is among the most celebrated of National Geographic staff photographers, fabled even among colleagues for his dedication. A journalism graduate of the University of Wisconsin whose skills were honed at the *Milwaukee Journal*, Stanfield joined the Geographic staff in 1967. For the next 28 years he worked in more than a hundred countries on 65 assignments whose subjects included chocolate, rats, gold, Burma, Genghis Khan, and an intimate glimpse of Pope John Paul II.

A Stanford graduate with a degree in geophysics, **GEORGE STEINMETZ** left his native Beverly Hills far behind when he spent two years hitchhiking through Africa. Best known for his exploration and science photography, Steinmetz sets out to reveal the few remaining secrets in our world today: remote deserts, obscure cultures, and new developments in science. He has shot more than 40 stories for *National Geographic* since 1989, often capturing innovative aerial shots from the heights of a drone or piloted paraglider.

In 1980, fresh out of the University of Virginia, **MARIA STENZEL**, ▸ unsure what to do with her life, turned up at National Geographic and accepted an entry-level job. Like many people, she quickly discovered that photojournalism was the ideal vocation. Through talent and hard work, she began publishing pictures, and two decades and more than two dozen assignments later, she has covered a wide range of subjects, but is especially enchanted with Antarctica.

Perhaps the most prolific National Geographic photographer of his era, **B. ANTHONY STEWART** (1904–1977) actually came to the Society in 1927 as the photo lab's bookkeeper. Soon enough, however, the Virginia native proved his proficiency with the camera, and before retiring in 1969, he had been long honored as the Society's chief photographer, having had many more pictures published than are even accounted for by the more than a hundred stories that carry his credit. Stewart never considered himself an artist, but his work epitomizes the early days of documentary photography. His images of the American West and life during the Great Depression are iconic historical records.

JAMES A. SUGAR was a young graduate of Wesleyan University whose talent with a camera had won him a coveted spot as a National Geographic photo intern in 1967. Two years later, the Baltimore native was back as a full-fledged contract photographer, and for the next 27 years he photographed a wide variety of subjects but concentrated mostly on technological pieces such as aviation and scientific ones on the sun and, even better, the universe.

JAMES T. TANNER (1914–1991) studied at Cornell University under the mentorship of Arthur A. Allen. In 1937 he went to the swampy Singer Tract in Louisiana to do his doctoral research on the nearly extinct Ivory-billed Woodpecker. The land owners did not take his recommendations for preserving the species, and Tanner's research remains the best documentation of these birds. Tanner went on to found the ecology program at East Tennessee State University and was a leader in national and state ornithological societies.

Born in rural North Carolina, **MEDFORD TAYLOR** joined the navy to see the world. After journalism school he saw a bit more of it while working for various newspapers and news magazines. In 1984, when he began two decades of freelancing for National Geographic, he saw quite a lot of it, shooting assignments on subjects as varied as Newfoundland and the Everglades, Madeira and the mountains of Central Asia, Iceland and the Australian outback.

WILLIAM THOMPSON began his art career as a painter before taking up the camera. He possesses both a Ph.D. in cultural anthropology and an unquenchable thirst for adventure, one that led him to track elephants across Asia and Africa and to live in the Himalaya for three years. Thompson shot several major stories on the region for *National Geographic* and created the first and only complete aerial coverage of Mount Everest for the 100-year anniversary issue of the magazine.

FREDERICK KENT TRUSLOW (1903–1978) was a businessman until age 53, when he resigned and began a new profession photographing birds. He wrote and photographed eight articles for *National Geographic*, and contributed to several other articles and books. His images also appeared in the magazines of the Audubon Society and the Cornell Lab of Ornithology. He died at age 75 from ALS, the illness known as Lou Gehrig's disease.

Brothers **BERT UNDERWOOD** (1862–1943) and **ELMER UNDERWOOD** (1859–1947) founded the company Underwood and Underwood in Kansas in 1881 to publish stereographs, which transported armchair travelers around the word. At its the peak, the company was producing 10 million "stereoviews" a year, including work by Herbert G. Ponting, Clarence White, and other major travel photographers of the time.

STEFANO UNTERTHINER took up photography as a hobby while growing up in a village in Italy. After earning a Ph.D. in zoology, he launched a career as an environmental journalist. Unterthiner tells the life stories of animals, often living for long periods in close contact with his chosen species.

DUNCAN USHER grew up among the wildlife of the Northumberland countryside in the United Kingdom. He was inspired to start painting and drawing the birds he saw after finding a book of waterfowl art as a teenager. Usher later developed a career as a professional photographer, for which his observant eye helps him capture the natural behaviors of birds and animals.

FRITS VAN DAALEN is a preeminent figure among Dutch bird photographers, with decades of experience in the field. In 1977, he founded one of the first unions of nature photographers to develop standards for responsible bird photography and share technical skills. The Natuur Fotografen Gilde still exists today with a large membership adhering to its code of ethics and the mission to promote conservation. Van Daalen also served as the Dutch editor for BirdLife and founded Foto Natura photo agency.

HUGO VAN LAWICK (1937–2002), known to millions in the 1960s and '70s as the Dutch husband of Jane Goodall, was a wildlife photographer and filmmaker who devoted his life to documenting the spectacular animal life of the Serengeti Plain. Born in Indonesia, he was reared in England before embarking on his African odyssey, which eventually garnered him eight Emmy Awards for his films.

RINIE VAN MEURS is an icebreaking adventurer, author, photographer, and guide. Van Meurs, who once took a job as a potato peeler to get on a ship's crew, has gone on more than 200 expeditions into the polar regions. He has published several books on polar bears and is a pioneer in ecotourism, leading cruises through the spectacular mountains and glacial bays of Greenland, the Norwegian archipelago of Svalbard, the geographical North Pole, the Falkland Islands, and Antarctica.

ANAND VARMA's ▼ films and photographs tell the story behind the science of complex issues. Varma worked on a variety of field projects while pursuing a degree in integrative biology and now uses photography to help biologists communicate their research. Varma has developed groundbreaking techniques to reveal small details invisible to the human eye and to stage shots that evoke an emotional response.

W. D. VAUGHN (dates unknown) joined National Geographic as a staff photographer in 1958, hired for his talent with Kodachrome and his healthy spirit of adventure. On one expedition, Vaughn made a 50,000-mile, five-month circuit of Africa to report on independence movements and the dissolving colonial powers. Another time, he climbed to the top of a suspension bridge that was about the height of the Washington Monument to catch a dizzying view of Lake Michigan as the wind whipped at his camera.

TOM VEZO (1947–2008) discovered birding and then bird photography while living on Long Island, New York. He eventually quit his job in business to immerse himself in the outdoors, traveling to hot spots across the United States and on to Antarctica and the Galápagos Islands to catch crystal-clear images and artistic compositions of animals presenting their natural behaviors.

LEWIS W. WALKER (1906–1971) was a naturalist, taxidermist, and exhibit designer for the American Museum of Natural History, in New York City, and later spent 17 years at the Arizona-Sonora Desert Museum. Walker set up a blind at a desert water hole that allowed him to photograph and deepen scientific knowledge of the diversity of animals that live in this sparse habitat. His work in Baja California helped lead to the establishment of the Rasa Island Wildlife Sanctuary.

CARLTON WARD, JR., is a conservation photographer and filmmaker focused on wild Florida. In 2010 he founded the Florida Wildlife Corridor project and has since trekked 2,000 miles during two National Geographic–supported expeditions to advocate for its protection. Ward has a master's degree in ecology. His photographs of the biological diversity of Gabon were exhibited at a United Nations reception.

Australian **OTHO WEBB** (dates unknown) pursued his photography with remarkable perseverance despite the technical limitations of the early 20th century and the nature of his subjects—often small insects and birds. A noted ornithological expert, Webb would sometimes build rickety tripods 35 feet in the air for a view into a nest.

VOLKMAR WENTZEL (1915–2006), originally of Germany, grew up in New York State and joined National Geographic in 1937, on the strength of his black-and-white photographs of Washington, D.C., at night. Although assignments took him all over the world, he is best remembered for his two-year odyssey covering India on the eve of its independence. Before retiring in 1985, he helped protect and preserve the Society's priceless collection of Autochromes.

STEPHEN WILKES's defining (ongoing) project is "Day to Night," epic cityscapes and landscapes recorded from a fixed camera angle for up to 30 hours. Blending these images into a single photograph takes months to complete. He spent most of 2017 on a *National Geographic* assignment to document the spectacle of bird migration. Wilkes has worked in photojournalism, fine art photography, and film and is based in New York City.

LAURA CRAWFORD WILLIAMS is a trained scientific illustrator as well as a wildlife photographer. Her pictures first appeared in *National Geographic* in 2007. Williams documents the fragile and irreplaceable beauty of the natural world, hoping her evocative images will spark wonder and intellectual curiosity.

MAYNARD OWEN WILLIAMS (1888–1963) quite simply opened the world for *National Geographic*. Hired in 1919 as the Society's first field correspondent, Williams, the first chief of the foreign editorial staff, wrote and photographed some 100 stories before his 1953 retirement. Roaming Europe, the Near East, the far reaches of Asia, the Arctic, and the Americas, he preferred cultivating "friendship, not adventure"—although he had plenty of both.

M. WOODBRIDGE "WOODY" WILLIAMS (1918–2012) was a writer and photographer for National Geographic who went on to serve as the chief photographer for the National Park Service. In what many consider a dream job, Williams documented the cultural and natural value of national parks, ranging from Utah's deep canyons to Alaska's mountain tops. Williams studied marine biology at Scripps Institution of Oceanography and was a member of the Explorers Club.

Jaguars, tigers, bears, snow leopards—as a boy in Indiana, **STEVE WINTER** dreamed of capturing them on film as a National Geographic photographer, and when in 1991 he began shooting for the magazine, he found himself having many close encounters with them. He has also covered such countries as Cuba and Myanmar. He has said of this dual focus, "I am fascinated by people and culture, and have a great love for the natural world." Winter is a conservation photojournalist and an expert on big cats. He once spent six months sleeping in a tent at minus 40°F to track snow leopards. He feels a great responsibility not only to show readers his subjects but also to give them a reason to care.

EDWIN L. "BUD" WISHERD (1900–1970) knew nothing about photography when in 1919 he joined the Geographic as a lab assistant—but he proved a quick study. Within a few years he had become one the first staff photographers to process Autochrome plates in the field. A pioneer of 35-mm Kodachrome in the 1930s, he became chief of the Society's photo lab, making it one of the finest such facilities in American publishing.

ART WOLFE has been practicing conservation photography for 50 years. His breathtaking collection includes many books, films, and awards. He travels nearly nine months out of the year, using his work to advocate for indigenous cultures and the environment, and teaches photography to inspire others to use their art to create change.

Born in Kolkata, India, **BELINDA WRIGHT** is an award-winning photographer and documentary filmmaker who has used the visual arts to expose and combat wildlife crimes in the country of her birth. In close partnership with authorities, and with grassroots environmentalists, Wright uses innovative monitoring technology to reduce human-animal conflict and to curb wildlife poaching and trafficking—with tremendous success. She is the founder and executive director of the Wildlife Protection Society of India (WPSI).

SVEN ZACEK is a freelance nature photographer who loves to play with light and movement. An Estonian native, Zacek thrives in chilling weather that keeps most people indoors. This fortitude has allowed him to capture the Finnish North draped in snow, the Northern Lights, and exquisite shots of the Great Gray Owl.

For many years the staff naturalist for the National Geographic Society, **PAUL A. ZAHL** (1910–1985) held both a master's and a doctorate in experimental biology from Harvard. The Illinois native made a specialty of natural history photography, and in 1958 he joined the National Geographic staff. His many articles and photographs for the magazine pivoted on subjects either very small (insects and sea creatures) or very large (the world's tallest tree, largest ant, and biggest flower).

CHRISTIAN ZIEGLER, a native of Germany, is a photojournalist specializing in natural history and science. He sees himself as a translator, interpreting the extraordinary beauty and scientific complexity of tropical ecosystems for the general public, and thereby raising awareness of the need for their conservation. Ziegler has been working on educational projects with museums and with environmental groups such as Conservation International and the World Wildlife Fund.

ARTISTS

JONATHAN ALDERFER, artist and editor, has contributed extensively to several editions of the *National Geographic Field Guide to the Birds of North America* and co-authored the sixth and seventh editions. He edited many birding books for National Geographic, has served on the Maryland/District of Columbia Bird Records Committee, and was an associate editor of the American Birding Association's magazine, *Birding*. Alderfer lives on the coast of Maine and specializes in seabirds.

FERNANDO G. BAPTISTA, a senior graphics editor for *National Geographic*, has elevated scientific visualization to high art. His illustrations and infographics have won global acclaim, including the Peter Sullivan Award, best known as "the Pulitzer for infographics." With an obsession for detail, Baptista typically works for months on a single design, creating sketches and models and traveling as far as Jerusalem or the Amazon rain forest to meet with experts, to translate complex concepts into compelling visuals.

Born in India, **ALLAN BROOKS** (1869–1946) traveled widely before and after his military service in World War I. While he was living in British Columbia in the 1930s, the National Geographic Society commissioned him to paint hundreds of illustrations for a series of 10 articles on bird families of the United States and Canada.

LOUIS AGASSIZ FUERTES (1874–1927) was born in Ithaca, New York, and graduated from Cornell University. After studying art with Abbott H. Thayer, he undertook many expeditions through the Western Hemisphere, making sketches and collecting bird skins. Fuertes illustrated more than 35 books and contributed paintings to more than 50 other publications. His works are in the collections of the Cornell Lab of Ornithology, the American Museum of Natural History, in New York, and the Academy of Natural Sciences, in Philadelphia.

Legend has it that **JOHN** (1804–1881) and **ELIZABETH GOULD** (1804–1841) met at the Aviary of the London Zoo. John was a taxidermist for the Zoological Society of London and a distinguished English ornithologist who published many seminal books on birds in the 19th century. Balancing her time as a wife and mother, Elizabeth was a largely self-taught artist who created more than 600 lithographs for their books and joined John on expedition to Australia.

HASHIME MURAYAMA ▲ (1878–1955) joined the staff of National Geographic at a time before color photography was common. Dedicated to pictorial precision in the representation of birds, fish, and insects, he was known to have counted the scales of a fish to ensure the accuracy of his paintings. An immigrant from Japan, Murayama saw his career cut short when his family was imprisoned in an internment camp during World War II. He never returned to fine art, though he continued scientific illustration to aid medical research.

JOHN P. O'NEILL was a consultant and artist for the monumental first edition of the *National Geographic Field Guide to the Birds of North America*. O'Neill holds a Ph.D. in zoology and served as director of the Louisiana State University Museum of Natural Science (1978–82), helping develop LSU into a leading ornithology research center. He has studied the birds of Peru for more than 40 years, often traveling by mule or canoe to access remote biodiversity hot spots. A bird species (*Nephelornis oneilli*) and a bird genus (*Oneillornis*) were named in his honor. O'Neill now paints full time.

Naturalist **ROGER TORY PETERSON** (1908–1996) was best known for his 50-volume Peterson Field Guides series. The first, a field guide to the birds of North America, is the forerunner to all future popular identification guidebooks. Peterson's talent for art developed during his childhood in parallel with his passion for nature. In 1984, to extend learning about nature to as many children as possible, he established the Roger Tory Peterson Institute of Natural History, in Jamestown, New York, which preserves his body of work.

Paintings by educator and illustrator **BARRON STOREY** have appeared in such publications as *Smithsonian*, *Scientific American*, and *American Heritage*. He contributed 14 cover illustrations to *Time* magazine between 1974 and 1984. Storey's mural of the South American rain forest is permanently installed in the American Museum of Natural History, in New York.

Trained as a biologist and an artist, **WALTER A. WEBER** ▼ (1906–1979) served as a staff illustrator for National Geographic for 22 years. His first position was with the Field Museum of Natural History, in Chicago. Weber's painting of Snowy Egrets was reproduced on a 1947 U.S. postage stamp issued upon the creation of Everglades National Park.

ADDITIONAL CONTRIBUTORS

MELINDA DICK is a member of YourShot, National Geographic's photography community.

SPECIES INDEX

Bold page numbers indicate illustrations.

ADDITIONAL CREDITS

(NGC) National Geographic Creative
(NGPA) National Geographic Photo Archive

Cover, Sven Začek/Wild Wonders of Europe; Back Cover, Walter A. Weber/NGC; Spine (top to bottom), Louis Agassiz Fuertes/NGC; Herbert G. Ponting/NGPA; Luis Marden/NGC; Stephen Wilkes; Bates Littlehales/NGC; Frans Lanting/NGC; Front Flap, Roe Ethridge, Pigeon, 2001; Back Flap, Joel Sartore/National Geographic Photo Ark/NGC; Endsheets, Oldesign/Shutterstock.

1, National Geographic Photo Ark/NGC; 2-3, NGC; 4, NGPA; 8-9, NGC; 10-11, NGPA; 12-13, NGC; 14-15, Roving Tortoise Photos; 16-17, NGC; 18-19, NGC; 20, NGPA; 23, NGPA; 24-5, NGC; 26, NGC; 32-3, NGPA; 34, NGC; 35, NGC; 36-7, NGC; 38, NGC; 40, NGC; 41, NGC; 42-3, NGC; 44-5, Mitchell Library, State Library of New South Wales, FL1551162; 46 (UP), NGC; 46 (LO), NGC; 47, NGC; 48, NGC; 49, NGC; 50-51, NGC; 52, NGC; 53, NGC; 54-5, NGPA; 56, NGC; 57 (UP), NGC; 57 (LO), NGPA; 58-9, NGC; 60, NGPA; 61, NGPA; 62, NGC; 63, NGC; 64, NGC; 65, NGC; 66-7, NGC; 68, NGPA; 69, NGPA; 70, NGC; 72-3, NGC; 74, NGC; 75, NGC; 76-7, NGPA; 78-9, NGC; 80 (UP), NGPA; 80 (LO), NGPA; 81, NGPA; 82, NGC; 84-5, NGPA; 86, NGPA; 87, NGPA; 88-9, NGC; 90, NGPA; 91, NGC; 92-3, NGPA; 94, NGC; 95, NGC; 96, NGC; 97, NGC; 98, NGPA; 100, NGC; 101, NGC; 102-103, NGPA; 104, NGPA; 105, NGPA; 106-107, NGC; 108, NGC; 109, NGC; 110 (UP), NGC; 110 (LO), NGC; 111, NGC; 112 (UP), NGC; 112 (LO), NGC; 113 (UP), NGC; 113 (LO), NGC; 114, NGC; 114-15, NGC; 116-17, NGC; 118-19, NGC; 120, NGC; 124-5, NGPA; 126, NGPA; 128-9, NGC; 130 (UP), NGC; 130 (LO), NGC; 131, NGPA; 132-3, NGPA; 134, NGPA; 135, NGPA; 136, NGC; 137, NGC; 138-9, NGPA; 140, NGPA; 141 (UP), NGPA; 141 (LO), NGPA; 142-3, NGPA; 144, NGC; 145, NGC; 146-7, NGC; 148, NGC; 150, NGPA; 151, NGPA; 152-3, NGC; 154, NGPA; 155, NGC; 156-7, NGPA; 158, NGC; 159, NGC; 160, NGC; 161, NGC; 162-3, NGC; 164, With the permission of The Museum of Vertebrate Zoology, University of California, Berkeley; 165, National Audubon Society, By Permission of Audubon; 166-7, NGC; 168 (UP), NGC; 168 (LO), NGC; 169, NGC; 170-71, NGC; 172, NGPA; 173, NGPA; 174, NGC; 176-7, NGC; 178, NGPA; 179, NGPA; 180-81, NGC; 182, NGC; 184-5, NGC; 186, NGC; 187, NGC; 188, NGC; 189, NGC; 190, NGPA; 191, NGPA; 192-3, NGC; 194 (UP), NGC; 194 (LO), NGC; 195, NGC; 196-7, NGC; 198, NGC; 199, NGC; 200, NGC; 202, NGC; 203, NGC; 204, NGC; 205, NGC; 206 (UP), NGPA; 206 (LO), NGPA; 207 (UP), NGPA; 207 (LO), NGC; 209, Minden Pictures/NGC; 210 (UP), Minden Pictures/NGC; 210 (LO), Minden Pictures/NGC; 212-13, NGC; 214-15, NGPA; 216, NGC; 220-21, NGPA; 222, NGC; 223, NGC; 224-5, NGC; 226, NGC; 227, NGPA; 228-9, NGC; 230, NGC; 231, NGC; 232-3, NGC; 234, NGC; 236, NGC; 237, NGC; 238-9, NGC; 240, NGC; 241, NGC; 244, NGC; 245, National Geographic Photo Ark/NGC; 246, NGC; 247, NGC; 248-9, NGC; 250, NGC; 251 (UP), NGC; 251 (LO), NGC; 252-3, NGC; 254, NGC; 255, NGC; 256, NGC; 257 (UP), NGC; 257 (LO), NGPA; 258-9, NGC; 260, NGC; 261, NGC; 262, NGC; 264 (UP), NGC; 264 (LO), NGC; 265, NGPA; 266, NGC; 267, NGC; 268-9, NGC; 270, NGC; 271, NGC; 272-3, NGC; 274, NGC; 275, NGC; 276, NGC; 277, NGPA; 278 (LO), NGC; 278 (UP), NGC; 279, NGC; 280-81, NGC; 282, NGPA; 283, NGC; 284-5, NGPA; 286, NGC; 287, NGC; 288-9, NGC; 290 (UP), NGC; 290 (LO), NGC; 291, NGC; 292-3, NGC; 294, NGC; 295, NGC; 298 (UP), NGC; 298 (LO), NGC; 300-301, NGPA; 302, NGC; 303, NGC; 304, NGC; 305, NGC; 306, NGC; 307, NGC; 308-309, NGC; 310, NGC; 312, Minden Pictures/NGC; 313, Minden Pictures/NGC; 314 (UP), Minden Pictures/NGC; 314 (LO), Minden Pictures/NGC; 315, Minden Pictures/NGC; 316-17, Minden Pictures/NGC; 318, Minden Pictures/NGC; 319, Minden Pictures/NGC; 320-21, NGPA; 322, Minden Pictures/NGC; 323, NGC; 324-5, NGC; 326, NGC; 328-9, NGC; 330, NGC; 331, NGC; 332 (UP), NGPA; 332 (LO), NGC; 333, NGPA; 334, NGC; 334-5, Minden Pictures/NGC; 336 (LO), NGC; 337 (UP), NGC; 337 (LO), NGC; 338, NGC; 339 (UP), NGC; 339 (LO), NGC; 340-41, NGC; 342, NGC; 346-7, NGC; 348, Minden Pictures/NGC; 349, NGC; 350-51, Minden Pictures/NGC; 352, Minden Pictures/NGC; 353, Minden Pictures/NGC; 354, NGC; 355 (UP), NGC; 355 (LO), NGC; 356-7, Minden Pictures/NGC; 358, NGC; 359, Minden Pictures/NGC; 360-61, NGC; 362, NGC; 364, NGC; 365, NGC; 366-7, Minden Pictures/NGC; 368, NGC; 369, NGC; 370-1, NGC; 372, Minden Pictures/NGC; 373, NGC; 374-5, NGC; 376, Minden Pictures/NGC; 377, Minden Pictures/NGC; 378-9, NGC; 380, NGC; 381, NGC; 382-3, Minden Pictures/NGC; 384, NGC; 385, NGC; 386, NGC; 387 (UP), NIS/Minden Pictures/NGC; 387 (LO), Minden Pictures/NGC; 388-9, NGC; 390, NIS/Minden Pictures/NGC; 391, NIS/Minden Pictures/NGC; 392, NaturalExposures.com; 394-5, Buiten-beeld/Minden Pictures/NGC; 396 (UP), NGC; 396 (LO), NGC; 397, Minden Pictures/NGC; 398-9, NGC; 400, NGC; 402 (UP), NGC; 403, NGC; 404-405, NGC; 406, NGC; 407, NGC; 408, Minden Pictures/NGC; 409, NGC; 412, Minden Pictures/NGC; 413, NGC; 414-15, Minden Pictures/NGC; 416, NGC; 417, NGC; 418-19, NGC; 420, Minden Pictures/NGC; 421, Minden Pictures/NGC; 422-3, NGC; 424 (LO), Solent News and Photo Agency; 425, NGC; 426, NGC; 427, NGC; 428-9, Minden Pictures/NGC; 430, Minden Pictures/NGC; 431, NGC; 432-3, NGC; 434, NGC; 435 (UP), National Geographic Photo Ark/NGC; 435 (LO), NGC; 436-7, NGC; 439, NGC; 440-41, NGC; 442, NGC; 444, NGC; 445, NGC; 446-7, NGC; 448 (UP), NGC; 449, NGC; 450, NGC; 451, NGC; 452-3, National Geographic Photo Ark/NGC; 454, Pigeon, 2001; 456, NGC; 458 (UP), NGC; 458 (LO), NGC; 459, NGC; 460-61, naturepl.com; 462, NGC; 463, NGC; 464-5, NGC; 466, NGC; 467, NGC; 468-9, NGC; 470, NGC; 471, NGC; 472, NGC; 473, NGC; 474-5, Hedgehog House/Minden Pictures; 476, National Geographic Photo Ark/NGC; 478-9, Photographed in cooperation with Lloyd and Rose Buck; 480 (UP), Photographed in cooperation with Lloyd and Rose Buck; 480 (LO), Photographed in cooperation with Lloyd and Rose Buck; 481, Photographed at the Goffin Lab, Messerli Research Institute, University of Veterinary Medicine, Vienna; 482-3, Photographed with permission of Audubon's Rowe Sanctuary; 484, NGC; 485, NGC; 486 (UP), NGC; 486 (LO), NGC; 487, NGC; 488 (LO), NGC; 488 (UP), NGC; 489 (UP), NGC; 489 (LO), NGC; 490-91, NGC; 491, NGC; 492, Minden Pictures/NGC; 493 (UP), NGC; 493 (LO), NGC; 494-5, National Geographic Your Shot; 496, NGC; 497 (UP), NGC; 497 (LO), NGPA; 498, NGC; 499 (LE), NGPA; 499 (RT), NGPA; 500 (UP), Minden Pictures/NGC; 500 (LO), NGC; 501 (LE), NGPA; 501 (RT), Minden Pictures/NGC; 502 (UP), NGC; 502 (LO), NGC; 503, Minden Pictures/NGC; 504 (UP), NGC; 504 (LO), NGC; 505, NGC; 506 (UP), NGC; 506 (LO), NGC; 507, NGPA; 508 (UP), NGC; 508 (LO), NGC.

A note on caption dates: All images that appeared in *National Geographic* carry the issue publication year. All other images are dated to the year they entered into the National Geographic Image Collection.

ACKNOWLEDGMENTS

We are indebted to the National Geographic Image Collection staff, especially Julia Andrews, Susie Riggs, and Michael Sutherland, for discovering and processing never-before-published images from the archives. Special gratitude is due to Michael Retter, for a keen research review, and to Mark Jenkins, for his insight into the storied past of the National Geographic Society. Finally, we thank our colleagues at the National Geographic Society, Jonathan Baillie, Beth Foster, Laura Bonnell, and Mike Ulica, for their support and involvement in this project.

Since 1888, the National Geographic Society has funded more than 13,000 research, exploration, and preservation projects around the world. National Geographic Partners distributes a portion of the funds it receives from your purchase to the National Geographic Society to support programs, including the conservation of animals and their habitats.

National Geographic Partners
1145 17th Street NW
Washington, DC 20036-4688 USA

Get closer to National Geographic explorers and photographers, and connect with our global community. Join us today at nationalgeographic.com/join.

To license images and illustrations from this book or to obtain a print, please contact the National Geographic Image Collection at:
E-mail: NatGeoCreative@NatGeo.com
www.NatGeoCreative.com

For information about special discounts for bulk purchases, please contact National Geographic Books Special Sales: specialsales@natgeo.com

For rights or permissions inquiries, please contact National Geographic Books Subsidiary Rights: bookrights@natgeo.com.

ISBN: 978-1-4262-1967-2

Printed in China

18/PPS/1

AS PART OF ITS COMMITMENT TO WILDLIFE AND A PLANET IN BALANCE, the National Geographic Society has funded the creation of *The Splendor of Birds*, to spread the word about the growing challenges facing birds, share artifacts from National Geographic's rich trove of archival media, and celebrate these magnificent creatures.

In 2018, National Geographic partnered with the Audubon Society, BirdLife International, and the Cornell Lab of Ornithology to celebrate Year of the Bird and encourage people around the world to take action to protect birds. As part of that effort, here are some tips for how you can help birds thrive:

1. **SAY NO TO SINGLE-USE PLASTIC.** Use reusable water bottles and grocery bags and commit to recycling household plastics, which can be harmful to birds.
2. **HELP BIRDS ON THEIR JOURNEY.** Window collisions are a major cause of bird deaths. By turning off lights at night you can help reduce these collisions.
3. **CHOOSE NATIVE PLANTS.** By landscaping with native species, your yard, garden, patio, or balcony becomes a vital recharging station for birds passing through and a sanctuary for nesting birds.

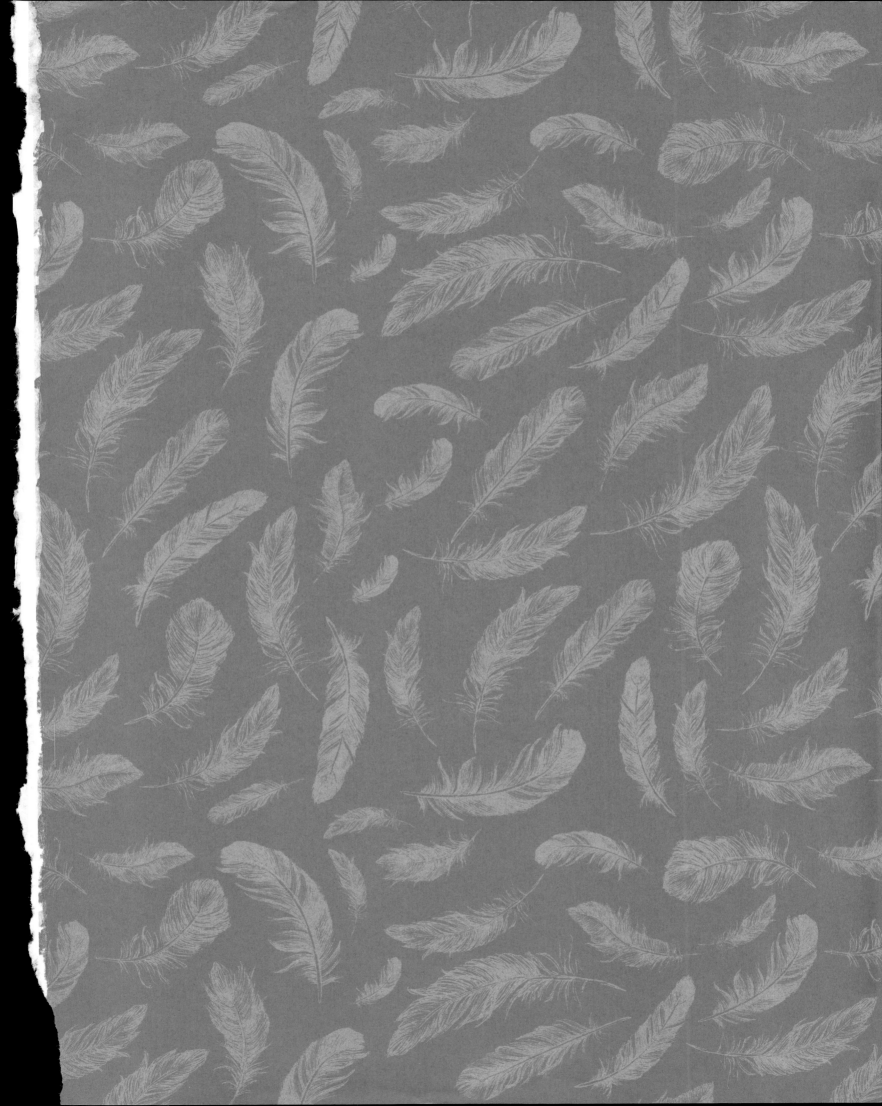

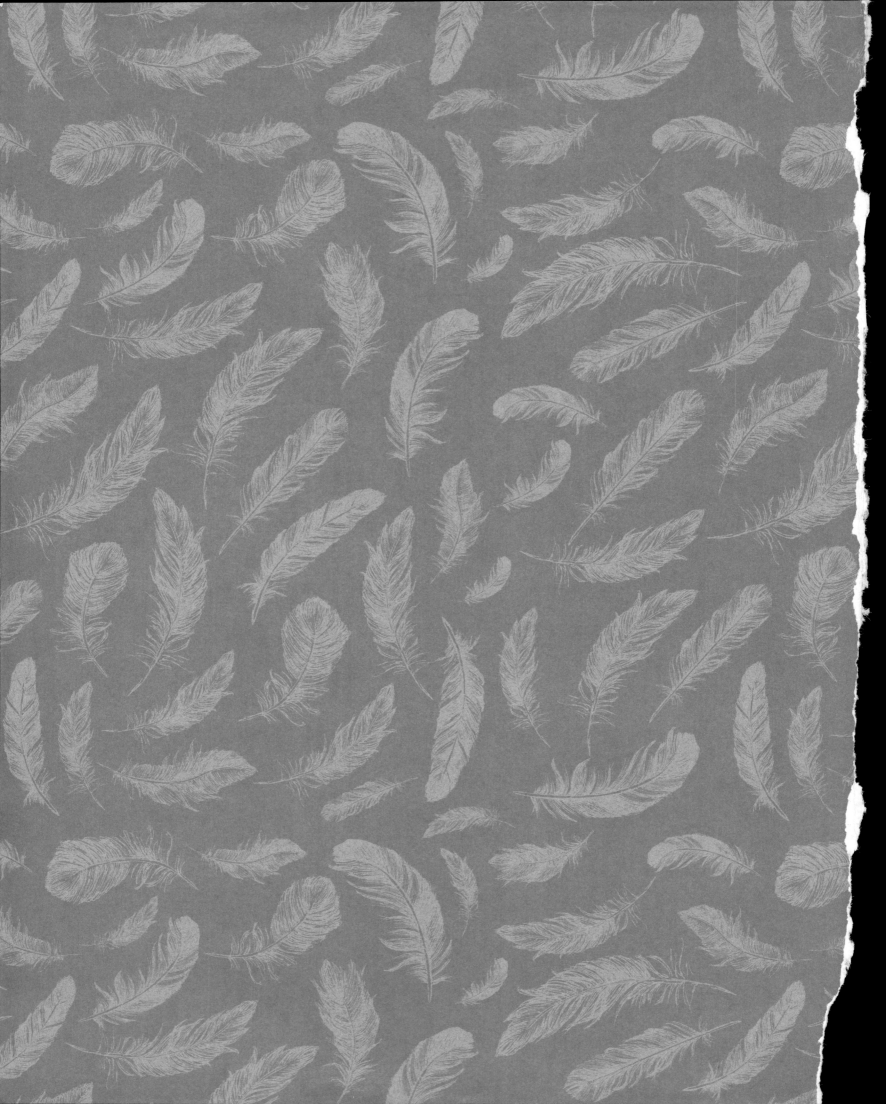